THE WAY OUT OF THE DEAD END
A Plea for Peace

D1808019

The Way Out of the Dead End

A PLEA FOR PEACE

by

Huschmand Sabet

Translated by
Patricia Crampton

GEORGE RONALD

OXFORD

GEORGE RONALD, Publisher
46 High Street, Kidlington, Oxford OX5 2DN

Original German-language edition
Der Weg aus der Ausweglosigkeit
© Copyright Seewald Verlag Dr. Heinrich Seewald GmbH & Co.
Stuttgart und Herford 1985
This translation © George Ronald 1986

British Library Cataloguing in Publication Data

Sabet, Huschmand
    The way out of the dead end: a plea for peace
    1. Peace
    I. Title   II. Der Weg aus der Ausweglosigkeit.
    English
    327.1'72   JX1944

    ISBN 0-85398-245-7
    ISBN 0-85398-240-6 Pbk

Phototypeset by Sunrise Setting, Torquay, Devon
Printed in Great Britain by Billing & Sons Limited, Worcester

Contents

Contents

Preface

Peace is Possible by Franz Alt was the inspiration for this participation in the peace debate, in response to his exhortation 'to seek with others a better path to peace'.

World-wide reflection on peace, the many publications on the subject, the arguments over the best way to achieve the goal – these are among the most encouraging events of our time. Just as the birds and buds of early spring herald its coming, so these contributions will sooner or later bring us closer to the great goal of peace. Never before in human history has such an intensive and general debate on world peace been initiated. The seriousness and the moral and human commitment evinced by these publications impress the reader with their authors' feelings and their resolute determination to indicate the ways and means which could lead to peace. I have learned much from the dialogues of the peace-makers.

Above all, I have been impressed and gladdened by the fact that in West Germany the Sermon on the Mount – as the expression of the highest religious standards – is playing an important part in the peace debate. Alt and many others are working to develop prescriptions for society and politics from the Sermon on the Mount. I can well understand this response to God's Word in

the depths of men's being, since I am profoundly convinced that the Holy Scriptures of all religions are an
inexhaustible source of encouragement on the way to
peace. Nevertheless, many experiences which will
be set out below have shown me that only the detailed
doctrines and principles of the youngest religion in
historical terms – the Bahá'í Faith – can help us to realise
the concrete significance of God's intentions for peace
in our time and how mankind can receive the blessing
of peace. In other words, I am convinced that we should
now regard all mankind as a human body, infected
with numerous diseases. Only a wise, divine doctor
to whom all the connections are visible can correctly
analyse the disease syndrome and prescribe the remedies
which will restore the patient's health. Bahá'u'lláh,
founder of the Bahá'í Faith, claims to be this divine
doctor for our time.

I do not intend to indulge in critical, or indeed
belligerent confrontation with the various movements,
each concerned from their own point of view about
peace; rather, my aim is to present the Bahá'í Teachings
as an auspicious and practical way to peace. That is why
this contribution to the current peace debate centres on
the Bahá'í Faith and at the same time tries to reveal the
connections with the necessary brevity.

I also assume a basic knowledge of the Bahá'í Faith;
there are several introductions to the subject and some are
listed in the Notes for those who require them.[1]

Since I am particularly concerned to lead the reader
directly to the source, I shall frequently be presenting
him with quotations from the writings of the leading
figures of the Bahá'í Faith, and on pages 111–25 I shall
introduce some of the personalities who encountered the

new faith or its founder and were affected in one way or another.

This book is based on the thesis that the dissemination of Bahá'u'lláh's doctrines and the increasing practical realisation of His world order support the establishment of 'formal peace' in the world and are the only means of enabling the 'peace of substance' to arise. 'Formal peace', described by Bahá'u'lláh as the 'Lesser Peace', will proceed from disruptions taking place on a scale inconceivable to us and is characterised by binding agreements between governments on the proscription of war. The 'Lesser Peace' will probably become a reality in the twentieth century itself. The 'peace of substance', described by Immanuel Kant as 'Eternal Peace', will take shape in the coming centuries increasingly, as the principles, laws and world order of Bahá'u'lláh make progress and help to realise the 'Most Great Peace', as He called it, on our planet. When we have the 'Most Great Peace' in view, we can work more effectively towards the 'Lesser Peace'.

In this light Jesus's Sermon on the Mount, that radiant jewel of the Gospels, is a promise of peace which is moving towards its fulfilment in the era that we have already entered.

Huschmand Sabet
Stuttgart, January 1985

The winds of despair are, alas, blowing from every direction, and the strife that divideth and afflicteth the human race is daily increasing . . .

. . . Soon will the present–day order be rolled up, and a new one spread out in its stead.

Bahá'u'lláh

ONE

The New Ark of God

Peace and Everyday Politics

When I am asked whether I am *for* or *against* the NATO dual track decision, or *for* or *against* 'Star Wars', I have to say, to many people's astonishment, that I cannot identify myself with any side at all, and that my religious attitude leads me to stand apart from any involvement with current politics. To many this is almost incomprehensible: they cannot understand why at such a critical point in current affairs the Bahá'ís do not take up a political stance.

The question is to what extent the politics of the day can perform any real service for peace at all. The highly contradictory insights and conclusions which Franz Alt's book title, *Peace is Possible*, has aroused in politicians and theologians, philosophers and laymen, Catholics and Protestants, make it obvious that ordinary politics have no solution in view. Every position has its 'good' arguments, but the 'good' arguments cancel each other out. This, the real dilemma on the road to the realisation of peace, explains why Werner Becker, taking stock of the peace debate, has called his book *The Conflict over Peace*.

To clarify the Bahá'í position it is helpful to recall the story of Noah and the Ark that saved him, as a recurrent divine principle. The metaphor of Noah's Ark points to a new way. After preaching for a long time to deaf ears God's Messenger gave up trying to restore a corrupt society; instead he summoned those who listened to him and believed in him into his ship of salvation. The old world founders, with all its pomp and corruption, while at the same time a new creation arises by divine intervention. We find basically the same development in the phenomenon of Moses. The new people of God are chosen and led into the desert and at last, after a lengthy process of education and enlightenment, to the Holy Land – a process comparable to that of Noah's Ark. Nor did Jesus restore the Roman Empire: God's new people took shape in dungeons and catacombs – as an alternative to the existing structures – in order to succeed to the proud Roman Empire corrupted by materialism and hedonism. A similar process can be observed in Islam. Muhammad fled from Mecca to Medina (Arabic for 'the city', symbolising the City of God). Here, as in Noah's Ark, the Prophet bestowed on his people that training and profoundly religious moulding which brought about the later evolution of the Faith and the growth of Islamic civilisation. Today, according to the religious convictions of the Bahá'ís, Bahá'u'lláh's world order is the divine Ark of Salvation.

By means of an example I shall try to portray the essence of that Ark of Salvation offered to us by Bahá'u'lláh. The whole of Alt's work demonstrates an honest attempt to derive solutions for a peaceful world from the injunction in the Sermon on the Mount to love our enemies. In the debate Alt is accused of failing to differentiate between personal enemies and enemies of the state. Many people believe that when Jesus spoke of loving our enemies he referred only to the first category, the personal enemy, but Alt extends the concept of loving our enemies to the enemies of the state, developing concepts which might prove dangerous to the protection of the community and the nation. There is little likelihood of consensus among Christians on this issue, because everyone is alone with his own interpretation and religious convictions. No interpretation is either able or authorised to act as a yardstick for the necessary common growth of conscience.

When I examine the writings of Bahá'u'lláh, however, I observe very few references to love of one's enemy. Instead we find quite new concepts which we encounter time and again: the unity of mankind and *universal love* are key concepts which will lead to the *Most Great Peace*. In the Bahá'í Faith the emphases are different. In God's new Ark the enemy, as an enemy of one's own race, nation or religion, is not admitted to exist. Bahá'u'lláh says:

Through each and every one of the verses which the Pen of the Most High hath revealed, the doors of love and unity have been unlocked and flung open to the face of men. We have erewhile declared – and Our Word is the truth – : 'Consort with the followers of all religions in a spirit of friendliness and fellowship.' Whatsoever hath led the children of men to shun one another, and hath caused dissensions and divisions amongst them, hath, through the revelation of these words, been nullified and abolished.

. . . Of old it hath been revealed: 'Love of one's country is an element of the Faith of God.' The Tongue of Grandeur hath, however, in the day of His manifestation, proclaimed: 'It is not his to boast who loveth his country, but it is his who loveth the world.' Through the power released by these exalted words He hath lent a fresh impulse, and set a new direction to the birds of men's hearts, and hath obliterated every trace of restriction and limitation from God's holy Book.[1]

This unconfined, universal love based on the unity of mankind and comprehensive justice within the Bahá'í world order might represent 'all truth'[2] as predicted by Jesus, to which we shall be led by the Promised One.

Udo Schaefer writes:

The commandment to love, rightly put forward by Christians as the *Summum bonum*, the quintessence of all morality, has had limitations imposed on it over the centuries: to people, race, religion or party. And where love is practised only within boundaries, it produces inward integration, but outward hatred. The wars of religion, the Crusades, the treatment of the Jews in Europe and particularly in Germany in our own century, or of the members of the black race in the United States and South Africa are examples of the way in which Christ's commandment to love one another has been distorted and limited in the course of history.[3]

This limitation of the commandment to love has caused me, personally, a great deal of concern. I could not and cannot understand that, for instance, there are memorials at church doors on both sides of the Rhine to the fallen soldiers who lost their lives for the *honour of the Fatherland*. This is not remembering the dead; it is erecting a glorified monument to nationalism. If the commandment to love is not limited to one's own country, militant nationalism appears as the image of a false god, and that is precisely why I am uneasy: images of false gods, erected in the forecourt of the houses of God.

In the context of individual ethics the doctrines of Bahá'u'lláh and the tenets of the Sermon on the Mount are identical. In connection with loving one's enemy in the sense of a personal enemy, 'Abdu'l-Bahá says:

Among the teachings of Bahá'u'lláh is one requiring man, under all conditions and circumstances, to be forgiving, to love his enemy and to consider an ill-wisher as a well-wisher. Not that he should consider one as being an enemy and then put up with him, or to simply endure him, or to consider one as inimical and be forbearing toward him. This is declared to be hypocrisy. This love is not real. Nay, rather, you must see your enemies as friends, ill-wishers as well-wishers, and treat them accordingly. That is to say, your love and kindness must be *real* . . . not merely forbearance, for forbearance, if not of the heart, is hypocrisy.[4]

I shall return later on to Bahá'u'lláh's world order and His doctrines, laws and commandments in connection with universal reconciliation. At the same time, I hope my readers will appreciate that this treatise does not include contributions to the peace debate stemming from the politics of the day.

Love and Justice

Christians who participate in the peace movement agree with me that the two elements of love and justice are both vital to the foundation of peace. Nor does justice receive short shrift in the Sermon on the Mount: 'Blessed are they which do hunger and thirst after righteousness, for they shall be filled.' 'Therefore I say unto you: except your righteousness shall exceed the righteousness of the scribes and Pharisees, ye shall in no case enter into the Kingdom of Heaven.'

Isaiah himself, greatest of the Jewish prophets, coined the significant phrase: 'And the work of righteousness shall be peace.'[5] In the carpet of peace the warp is love, love of neighbour, universal love, but the woof is justice and order, which as regards world peace means world order. That is the only way to prevent the abuse of love by tyrants and oppressors. Only universal love enfolded in universal justice can spread a universal, lasting peace.

That is why the aspect of justice in the world, and hence a just world order, must not be excluded from our considerations, in the hope that somehow, at some time, it will be spontaneously generated. When we speak of universal justice, however, we are consciously or unconsciously assuming something fundamental, namely the unity of mankind.

The concept of the 'unity of mankind' is really the key concept of the Bahá'í Faith. World peace, insofar as it deserves the name, is a product, or more properly a fruit of the *unity of mankind*. From fear and need we have accustomed ourselves in recent years to seeing world peace principally in terms of the hope of a disarmament treaty between the Great Powers and we have therefore given little consideration to the other important aspects of world peace. For instance, if we want to remove hunger from the world, we must take world-wide responsibility for all the starving. This partnership with the starving presumes that we accept the principle of the *unity of mankind* in this area. The situation is exactly the same if we want to eradicate illiteracy world-wide, or help the five hundred million and more of the sick in the Third World who are eking out an existence in misery, poverty and ignorance. Even in the religious sphere these barriers and prejudices can be finally removed only if we regard all the major religions as endowments of God, if we inwardly experience the *unity of God's Messengers* and value their standing as the enlightened universal teachers of mankind.

New Key Truths

Three of the basic doctrines of the Bahá'í Faith contribute to the removal of religious prejudices and the world-wide establishment of a spirit of valuation and recognition of other religions that far transcends mutual tolerance. These three are:

1. The unity of religions;
2. Progressive divine revelation;
3. The relativity of religious truth.

The doctrine of the *unity of religions* is also reflected in the Sermon on the Mount, where Jesus reveals an aspect of Himself in the words: 'Think not that I am come to destroy the law, or the prophets: I am not come to destroy, but to fulfil.' The sweep of the *unity of religions* covers all the revelations from Adam to Jesus and from Jesus to the Promised One who is to come with a new name,[6] that is, the *unity of the religion* of God in past, present and future. Jesus identifies the coming revelation for the establishment of the Kingdom of Peace with His own mission so fully that He simply speaks of His own return.

Progressive divine revelation and the *relativity of religious truth* are also Biblical. When Jesus looks back on the earlier revelation, He speaks as He does several times in the Sermon on the Mount: 'Ye have heard that it was said

. . . But *I* say unto you . . .' When Jesus addresses His faithful followers on the subject of the next revelation, He says: 'I have yet many things to say unto you, but ye cannot bear them now. How be it when he, the Spirit of truth is come, he will guide you into all truth: for he shall not speak of himself, but whatsoever he shall hear, that shall he speak: and he will show you things to come.'[7] Christian commentaries link this passage of the Scripture with the phenomenon of Pentecost; however, the fact that the words used are that the Spirit of truth 'shall hear', 'shall speak: and . . . will show you things to come', seems more likely to indicate a figure to appear in the future.

I know that Christians have difficulty in accepting Islam into this *unity of religions*. Perhaps from the current Christian standpoint, with a few ifs and buts, more 'traces of revealed truth' – as Pope John XXIII put it – can be found in Buddhism, Hinduism and Zoroastrianism than in Islam, although a recent article in a Catholic family magazine carried a photograph of Pope John Paul II with the Mufti of Syria, under the headline: 'I read the Qur'án every day too.'[8] The understanding of the *unity of religions* will also cost Christians some conscious effort. When we consider that not so very long ago the other founders of religions were regarded as false prophets and their followers as heathens, we can observe a thoroughly satisfactory development in the right direction. All the same, I have the feeling that many Christians are unwilling to concede to Islam what they unreservedly allow to Christianity. When so-called Christians commit crimes, this has nothing to do with Jesus of Nazareth, but when so-called Muslims commit atrocities this is regarded as the fruit of Islam and condemned as such. As a rule certain value judgements then follow: the God of Christianity is a loving God, while the God of the Muslims or the Jews is an avenging God. Judgements of this kind make me comment ironically that the God of the Protestants is a God of freedom and the God of the Catholics a God of order, whereas in reality the attributes of God in all the world's revealed religions are very similar. But because the members of the various religions were always intent on *dissociation* and not on unity, they did everything they could to build up barriers and denounce one another.

Does Our Civilisation have a Future?

It is clear from an analysis of the contributions to the peace debate[9] that fear and despair have largely destroyed the earlier confident expectation of the triumph of peace. People are increasingly aware of the sickness of the world. When Western civilisation was preparing to become a world civilisation, something went wrong. The destructive forces are evidently stronger than suspected and are gradually going out of control. There is only limited agreement about the causes of the present crisis and practically no consensus on the remedy. Modern man in East and West has to the greatest possible extent abjured his spiritual nature and thus declared himself a 'higher animal'. This is why he is incapable of recognising that his happiness, indeed his survival, are dependent on harmony between his own will and the Will of the Creator. Since, however, modern man has rent the bonds between himself and God, it is hardly surprising if he is punished for his wilfulness and rejection of the Divine Will.

On the other hand, the sufferings we have so tragically incurred are invisibly creating the necessary conditions for the unification of mankind. Despite all that stubbornness, God has not abandoned mankind. Bahá'u'lláh revealed: 'The winds of despair are, alas, blowing from every direction, and the strife that divideth and afflicteth the human race is daily increasing. The signs of impending convulsions and chaos can now be discerned, inasmuch as the prevailing order appeareth to be lamentably defective.'[10]

Shoghi Effendi, Guardian of the Bahá'í Faith, describes the radical changes on earth and the goal which mankind, unknown to most people, is approaching:

The ages of its infancy and childhood are past, never again to return, while the Great Age, the consummation of all ages, which must signalize the coming of age of the entire human race, is yet to come. The convulsions of this transitional and most turbulent period in the annals of humanity are the essential prerequisites, and herald the inevitable approach, of that Age of Ages, '*the time of the end*', in which the folly and tumult of strife that has, since the dawn of history, blackened the annals of mankind, will have been finally transmuted into the wisdom and the tranquillity of an undisturbed, a universal, and lasting peace, in which the discord and separation of the children of men will have given way to the world-wide reconciliation, and the complete unification of the divers elements that constitute human society.

This will indeed be the fitting climax of that process of integration which, starting with the family, the smallest unit in the scale of human organization, must, after having called successively into being the tribe, the city-state, and the nation, continue to operate until it culminates in the unification of the whole world, the final object and the crowning glory of human evolution on this planet. It is this stage which humanity, willingly or unwillingly, is resistlessly approaching.

It is for this stage that this vast, this fiery ordeal which humanity is experiencing is mysteriously paving the way. It is with this stage that the fortunes and the purpose of the Faith of Bahá'u'lláh are indissolubly linked . . . It is the structure of His New World Order, now stirring in the womb of the administrative institutions He Himself has created, that will serve both as a pattern and a nucleus of that world commonwealth which is the sure, the inevitable destiny of the peoples and nations of the earth.

Just as the organic evolution of mankind has been slow and gradual, and involved successively the unification of the family, the tribe, the city-state, and the nation, so has the light vouchsafed by the Revelation of God, at various stages in the evolution of religion, and reflected in the successive Dispensations of the past, been slow and progressive. Indeed the measure of Divine Revelation, in every age, has been adapted to, and commensurate with, the degree of social progress achieved in that age by a constantly evolving humanity.[11]

TWO

Why Not Christianity?

Scepticism about Peace

One of the greatest problems on the road to peace is that although people long for it they are in reality unable seriously to believe that it is possible. As if walking in a maze, they keep on bumping into walls, unable to find the way out. These are some of the objections one hears:

– Even in families there is no peace, so how can one believe in a universal peace?
– Throughout the history of mankind there have been wars. What entitles us to assume that this will no longer be so in the future?
– Man is aggressive by nature: his essential nature demands conflicts and wars. Even religions have been quite unable to alter the nature of man in the past, so why should this be possible in the future?
– It has constantly been observed in history that unity was achieved thanks to the existence of a common enemy. Hence universal peace is a Utopia.
– It is impossible to create unity in Europe today. It is impossible to create unity between Protestants and

Catholics. How then are all the peoples, all the religions, all the nations supposed to achieve peace?

– In the developing countries people have no desire to work hard. The material for conflict is therefore always available.

– World unity cannot help leading to world dictatorship.

– The unity of the world would inevitably lead to the loss of identity of the peoples, countries and religions.

Even in the nuclear age there are still those who see something positive in war by old tradition, somewhat in the manner of Heraclitus: war is the father of all things, king of all things, 'some it makes gods, others human beings, others slaves, others free men'.[1]

Moltke says: 'Without war the world would be bogged down in materialism.'[2]

Even those concerned with education for peace are not free of pessimism and scepticism:

As well as defining the concept of peace, however, this survey leads to an additional insight which is decisive for practical peace education: the way to a world-wide peaceful order, in which there would be no more war as an organised, collective form of the use of power, is – seen from today's standpoint – infinitely long . . . paradoxically the definition of the concept of peace accordingly leads to its being immediately abandoned and to the distant goal being given up as a methodical approach to education for peace.[3]

The Time was not Fulfilled

To Christians engaged in the peace debate it may seem strange that the Bahá'í Faith should see the establishment of the 'peace of substance' as its own spiritual mission, rather than that of Christianity. The reason is simple: at the time of Christ's revelation the time for peace had not yet been fulfilled.

All the statements and prophecies about the establishment of the Kingdom of God on earth refer to the Second Coming of Christ, to a mighty revelation still to come. Christ's revelation directs attention to the redemption of the individual. We find no reference in the Gospels to the unification of mankind as a whole, or to the unity of nations. At that time large portions of the globe were unexplored and the unity of mankind could be neither announced nor established. Jesus was not addressing individual human beings as the foundation stones of an indivisible, comprehensive unity. Bahá'u'lláh explains the fine distinction between His Dispensation and the Dispensation of Christ: 'Truly, He [Jesus] said: "Come ye after Me, and I will make you to become fishers of men." In this day, however, We say: "Come ye after Me, that We may make you to become the quickeners of mankind."'[4]

Whether and to what extent the Sermon on the Mount can offer us the system of values necessary to the foundation of a general peace, is and remains controversial, but we could look back from the present day to the history of Europe and Christianity, and ask ourselves critical questions:

1. Why, in the two-thousand-year history of Christianity, are there no instances of peoples in the Christian civilisation being able to live long together in peace, according to the maxims of the Sermon on the Mount?

2. If peace was not possible in Europe when Christianity was the all-determining and moulding force, when the great Church governed the whole of private and public life, how can one expect a secularised world, turned half-

atheist, half largely areligious, to attain a lasting peace through the teachings of the Sermon on the Mount?

3. Are there structures for a world order deriving its motivation from the Sermon on the Mount? This question is particularly important because, as we have already said, no society – of whatever type and size – can dispense with the principle of justice for the sake of its pacification. The Sermon on the Mount, however, describes the ethos of the individual and apparently gives scarcely any guidance for structures embracing the whole of mankind and protecting the community from abuses. It is still impossible to expect everyone in the world to turn into angels overnight, and hence to dispense with law, justice and an order that protects the 'good' from the 'bad'.

Secularisation as the Establishment of Peace?

Societies in the Christian civilisation have undoubtedly undergone an irreversible secularisation manifesting itself in a variety of stubbornly competitive ideological schools. Fascism, National Socialism, Liberalism, Socialism and Communism are some of the manifestations of this process of secularisation.

Secularisation has penetrated the general awareness to such an extent that people unconsciously identify with one or other of its schools. However much they may envisage a divine State on earth, to many people a radical new beginning seems unnatural, pointless, indeed impossible.

From the moral standpoint one can identify the most important current forms of secularisation of Christianity as 'elbow' ideologies – ideologies intent on making room for themselves in society. In one case the elbows belong to the state, in the other to the individual. According to the camp one has adopted, one of these is perceived, the other suppressed.

Victory over secularisation by an original religion, by a new divine revelation, is not considered at all. Like Münchhausen, mankind wants to drag itself out of its misery by its own topknot, by means of one ideology or another, so it should be no surprise when pessimism and scepticism keep gaining ground. Karl Jaspers is so pessimistic that he insists that rule by dictatorship is essential to any form of world government.[5] It is interesting that Becker observes that even in the democracies decision-making in a crisis cannot be controlled or influenced by the people.[6] Jonathan Schell also speaks in connection with a world government of a 'desperate and unwanted plunge'.[7]

I cannot understand this. I propose a model to clarify the problem: suppose that owing to some kind of catastrophe the whole world is destroyed except for the USA, why should the government of the United States, which harbours peoples of every possible race and culture, necessarily turn into a dictatorship?

New Basic Values are Needed

Where does this negative attitude come from? Why are world government and world dictatorship constantly equated either consciously or unconsciously? I believe the reason is the lack of a spiritual basis for the birth and development of new political culture, for the establishment of a just world government where we can see our ideals and moral standards taken into account.

Jonathan Schell is right:

The peace movement, like the world as a whole, is in need of proposals for action which are commensurate with the hopes that it has raised, and are answerable to the moral standards it uses to measure present policies.[8]

We are travelling down a long, dark tunnel, afraid that in the daylight at the end we shall find we are slaves. The world-wide concern of Bahá'ís over the selection and choice of the decision-makers and the way in which consultation[9] should take place at all levels is extraordinarily important to the creation of a new political culture. This constitutes an important contribution to peace, for the Bahá'í Faith is also aware that peace does not come cheaply.

New strategies are needed to solve problems and take decisions, as well as new psychological equipment for the human being, both individually and collectively. As human beings we are neither equal nor agreed in our goals, expectations, hopes and priorities, nor will becoming Bahá'ís make us so. What we receive are basic values, a long-term goal formulated in general terms, the Word to point the way in our life struggle, and the Bahá'í Administrative Order as a training ground for the necessary new psychological and social structures.

So when Bahá'ís call for a world government, a world court of arbitration and other international institutions, they do so in the context of the laws and guidelines revealed by Bahá'u'lláh, to which they try to give model form in the Bahá'í institutions.

In this work Bahá'ís can give proof of world-wide practical experience which is available to everyone. Rather like in a laboratory, Bahá'ís are already working in the context of the new structures in tens of thousands of places all over the world, striving towards something they perceive as their particular task. All those concerned with world peace would be well advised to pay due attention to the work of Bahá'ís in the new 'Ark of God': unity, from this standpoint, is first and foremost the ability to tolerate each other in all our variety, to learn to understand the otherness of our neighbour and love it as the expression of divine reality,[10] consciously to recognise and assess values and then to make decisions with less and less loss of content, in social institutions in particular. The associated struggle, the great emphasis on willingness to learn, fear of God, civil courage, intellectual independence and inner freedom of the individual and the obedience born of it, are essential contributions of the Bahá'í culture to peace.

Peace through a Conclave of Religions?

Franz Alt, in his book *Peace is Possible*, criticises the lukewarm faith of many Christians and theologians because they make the commandment to love one's enemy relative, and to that extent declare Jesus to be incompetent. He criticises the fact that many princes of the Church and theologians do not take the words of Christ seriously enough, but at the same time he believes that a peace conclave of the religions would assist the cause of peace.[11] A common Council of Religions means so much to him that he devotes a whole chapter to it. Others such as Carl-Friedrich von Weizsäcker also advocate this system.

Religions affect people at the root of their self-image. They profoundly influence the human picture of the world. Religions touch man at the deepest ground of his existence and are distinguished from any philosophies or ideologies by the manner in which they do this. Only the religions provide definitive answers to the question of purpose, supply reliable and absolute yardsticks, and indicate final goals. And yet I am sceptical about the possible outcome of such a conclave of religions. My reason is that the socio-practical laws of the religions, to put it bluntly, are out of date for the needs of today. We could go through the Mosaic and Islamic laws in detail and most enlightened observers would agree that these laws are out of date and must be either abandoned or reformed. The same applies to the legal structure and caste laws of Hinduism. Christianity has few social laws of its own and many believe that the Mosaic laws, insofar as they are not expressly annulled, also apply to and are binding on Christians. However this may be, even the few social laws expressly established in the Gospels are not suitable for today. We have only to think of the prohibition of usury and divorce.

Therefore a kind of reformation must take place within all religions. Experiences through the millennia have shown, however, that reforms carried out by people never lead to a new unity – on the contrary, they have brought further breaches and fragmentation. Such reforms were and are the primary cause of sects arising within religions.

Apart from the fact that there is obviously not enough commitment available today to achieve a unified view in such a vital question as that of world peace within a single church, let alone among all the religions, I wonder who should be authorised to invalidate the laws decreed by the founders of the traditional religions. For instance: 800

million Muslims recognise the requirement to wage
'Holy War' as a divine commandment. If an assembly of
religions is convened, an authority of equal rank with
Muhammad will have to rescind the Holy War
requirement once and for all. If not, every discussion on
the total ostracism of all wars would appear to a Muslim
as an incapacitation of Muhammad.

Bahá'u'lláh rescinded the commandment to wage
Holy War. This is more than reformation. Every Bahá'í
knows, thanks to the recent revelation of Bahá'u'lláh,
what God's intentions are for humanity and what
practical steps they call for.

Many Christians, therefore, cherish no hopes of peace
for the future. They argue that if Jesus himself did not
bring world peace, how much less can we expect it in our
times. They overlook the fact that Jesus did not come to
inaugurate the era of peace; he came to proclaim it.
Christ's words 'I came not to bring peace, but a sword',
actually characterise the age of Christianity. It is the
Promised One, as the 'Prince of Peace'[12] who rings in the
era of universal peace.

The Kingdom of God on earth, the principal plea of the
Lord's Prayer, Jesus's only prayer, has an unreal
dimension for many Christians. Consciously or unconsciously, two things are observed:
1. It is virtually inconceivable that we shall in practice
experience the Kingdom of God on earth, especially as,
according to many theologians, this kingdom of peace is
an apocalyptic concept.
2. It is virtually inconceivable that we can contribute
anything in practice to its inception and realisation.

But if this were the case, and if we human beings were
really allowed to play virtually no role in the inception of

the kingdom of peace, it would be difficult to see for what reason, whenever we pray in the way Jesus wished, we should direct our consciousness towards this and sensitise our religious sentiment in this way.

Bahá'ís support the view that the Kingdom of God on earth represents a gift from God to man, as indeed does the whole of creation, but that it will be built with us and amongst us in a new age – which has already dawned – by the Prince of Peace, by means of a fresh outpouring of the Divine Will. The Kingdom of God on earth, according to Bahá'ís, describes a unified, peaceful world, in which political life is guided by ethical maxims and power is the handmaiden of justice. Hence the Kingdom of God on earth is a framework set up by God for man, into which we have to grow. Formerly the time was not ripe for this, but now, according to the Bahá'í teachings, the time is fulfilled.

Bahá'ís believe that the World Order, the doctrines and commandments of Bahá'u'lláh, constitute the elements of the Kingdom of God on earth and conform to all the spiritual and moral claims.

Optimism and Sin

The peace debate in Germany has an optimistic tenor, articulating the fact that peace is possible: that man is educable to peace. This precisely corresponds with our position, but in the treatment of sin there are contradictions: if sin is not separation from the Divine – as darkness is lack of light – if sin in the Christian view leads an incalculable life of its own, whence then comes the certainty that we shall ever achieve world peace in the future?

The idea of absolute sin is unknown to Bahá'ís. 'Abdu'l-Bahá says: 'All sin comes from the demands of nature, and these demands, which arise from the physical qualities, are not sins with respect to the animals, while for man they are sin. The animal is the source of imperfections, such as anger, sensuality, jealousy, avarice, cruelty, pride; all these defects are found in animals, but do not constitute sins. But in man they are sins.'[13] And he further states: 'The physical nature is inherited from Adam, and the spiritual nature is inherited from the Reality of the Word of God, which is the spirituality of Christ. The physical nature is born of Adam, but the spiritual nature is born from the bounty of the Holy Spirit; the first is the source of all imperfection, the second is the source of all perfection. The Christ sacrificed himself so that men might be freed from the imperfections of the physical nature, and might become possessed of the virtues of the spiritual nature.'[14]

The commandments and teachings in every revelation set a standard of goodness; to depart from them is sin. This means that good and evil are not fixed in their value once for all, but are themselves subject to development. For instance, everything which is opposed today to the unity of mankind and world peace is 'sin' in the eyes of the Bahá'ís.

Yet Christian theologians involved in the peace debate are hampered by old ideas about sin which theology itself has shown to be questionable.[15] Neither Franz Alt nor Manfred Hättich, a Catholic Professor of Politics at the University of Munich, can completely abandon the idea of man broken by sin; both plead for a stronger sense of sin among the followers of all religions. And to many theological critics this position is even too liberal, its picture of man too optimistic. Hättich speaks of the 'broken man'.[16] What can he mean by this in connection with the goal of peace? In my view, peace on earth is a structure that exhibits many individual parts, many spaces, many aspects and segments, and whose architect is the Divine Revealer. Are we condemned, according to the theory of the 'broken man', never to realise world peace? What detail in the process of the realisation of peace would this standpoint exclude? And on what grounds? Does this breakpoint also affect scientific progress, or is it limited in its practical effects only to the social and inter-human sphere?

Two comments may be permitted:

1. The historical objection that humanity has never lived in peace cannot validly be projected into the future; up to a certain moment we had never been on the moon, and that is now a reality. Moreover, man has shown a willingness to integrate. He has evolved from hunter and gatherer to 'civilised man' and organised himself in larger and larger societies. Why should that come to a sudden end?

2. Man is called to higher things and will fulfil them with God's help. Hermann Hesse defines this process quite clearly in his book *Steps*. To exclude the possibility of progress for mankind in specific areas is unscientific and contradicts the spirit of the Sermon on the Mount. 'Be ye therefore perfect, even as your Father which is in heaven is perfect.'[17]

The whole debate takes me back to the 1950s. When I came to a German university in 1950, owing to my Bahá'í education I was filled with ideas about the unity of man and peace. After the catastrophe of the Second World War I thought that the German people had paid so much blood-money for their nationalist mania that they must be wholly accessible to the idea of world unity and a just world order, but in numerous debates I met with the opposite outlook. Whenever and wherever conversations and talks took place on the subject of world peace, pessimism became apparent. Most Christians took the doctrine of original sin as the basis of their argument, claiming that everyone was saddled with original sin from conception and birth, and was incapable of overcoming that barrier through his own efforts. Accordingly the idea of a just peace in this world was nothing but an optimistic Utopia which failed to consider our inadequacy, our captivity in original sin.[18] Thus perceived, there is no possibility of divine grace, for progress and for the redemption of mankind. This negative attitude was partly responsible for the loss of thirty precious years of work for peace.

We can be thankful that scarcely anyone now speaks of the compulsion to sin – in the sense of the classical doctrine of original sin – in connection with peace. There must be a way out, where world peace can be found. For a decade or a generation, or even two or three generations, if you like, mankind may be lucky and avoid global war between the superpowers, but in the long term our chances of survival cannot depend on accident, they must have a solid foundation in ourselves.

Franz-Josef Rinsche, for instance, opposes Alt's theory with some very serious arguments. His plea on behalf of his way out of the present crisis does not, however, justify the claim of his book: *Only Thus is Peace Possible*. He writes: 'Here, however, we must proceed from the realistic expectation that it will never be possible to move all the heads of state in this world to a credible and reliable renunciation of force for all time.'[19] The consistent conclusion from this appreciation of the situation, and the 'realistic' possibilities for humanity, remind us of the man playing Russian roulette with a pistol to his own temple. Because he is attached to life he puts his hopes in the magazine with the least possible active ammunition and the least chance of a fatal shot. No one even tries to work out whether and how the pistol can finally be thrown away. No mathematician would wager a penny on the chances of this man's survival, for one day the deadly shot will be fired – perhaps sooner rather than later. Despite constant repetition one thing is constantly forgotten: in spite of the assertions to the contrary in some studies, the human race can be wiped out by total war on this planet. We need a draft from God's hand of the plan of heaven on earth, in order to be able to realise it step by step, with God's help. Whether we want to or not, we live in an age of 'all or nothing'.

Peace and the Human Image in the Religions

The followers of the various religions always have their specific problems in entering under the new roof of the unity of mankind and thus consciously into the new era. The Hindus see humanity through the spectacles of the caste system, that intelligent alternative to slavery. The Jews are greatly influenced in their religion by the distinction between Jews – the elect of God – and non-Jews. In addition to the distinction between Muslims and non-Muslims as regards legal rights, the Muslims have to overcome the commandment to wage Holy War.[20]

It seems to me that many Christians cannot conceive of peace. Without knowing it they think within definite theological structures characterised by pessimism and scepticism. In many cases they do not consider peace to be possible or willed by God in the here and now, but only in the hereafter. They argue that it is presumptuous and naive to expect heaven on earth. The possibility of realising peace by stages (as with every kind of progress in human history) is excluded.

Gerhard Borné, author of *The Sermon on the Mount and Peace*, to whom the commandments of the Sermon on the Mount in our time are the *ultima ratio*, writes on the question of a realisable peace thus:

This kingdom of God, this imminent expectation was simply an idea, a Utopian hope, whose literal realisation is inconceivable. This kingdom never came in the originally expected sense nor will it ever come.[21]

The following quotations from the opinion of the German Bishops on the subject of peace[22] remind us of a driver who is simultaneously accelerating and braking:

The Christian faith has always emphasised that perfect peace cannot be achieved until the world comes to an end and history is over. That is why it is always sceptical of programmatic promises of 'eternal peace'.

The advance of civilisation, people think, even if it were to remain a crisis-ridden process, will attain to a state of world peace based on good sense and morality, common economic interests ('commercialism') and the brotherly unity of mankind. The conditions for this have to be created: intellectual and religious prejudices and social paternalism have to be overcome, a harmony of economic interests to be discovered, abuses in social life to be eliminated. Eternal peace will become – and this is something new – an historically feasible programme which can be realised under the constant guidance of good sense together with a legitimate natural necessity.

On the contrary, the greatest scepticism, indeed contradiction is called for vis-à-vis those doctrines of salvation which assume that mankind is going to develop to a condition of perfected humanity and preparedness for peace.

The Gospel gives us the assurance that our activities on behalf of peace are not in vain.

Ultimate peace will not be gained in the form of any kind of new political order.

Even if the knowledge and experience of a broken nature are part of the Christian interpretation of man, the Christian will not be content with this bleak knowledge. His faith urges him on to a fresh preparedness for peace which will not be discouraged by disappointments, defeats and opposition.

In direct opposition to this we have Bahá'u'lláh's absolutely clear message that the Lord of the world has come and that His will is to bestow peace on mankind. But unless mankind believes in the goal of a lasting world peace and strives for it constantly in a spirit of sacrifice and devotion, never allowing himself to be discouraged by setbacks, the goal is unattainable.

The late Protestant theologian Kurt Hutten distinguishes thus between the Christian and Bahá'í doctrines:

The Bahá'í doctrine believes in man's natural goodness and ability to improve because it does not take sin seriously . . . What then is the good of the Cross in this optimistic faith which knows only a loving God and a mankind which, though it errs, is well-intentioned and capable of correction?[23]

Then Hutten draws the conclusion that the optimistic Bahá'í image of mankind is an illusion.[24] On similar grounds John Butterworth[25] also distinguishes the Christian from the Bahá'í teachings for the American public.

When it comes to thinking about peace, Hättich's attitude is typical of many Christians:

For that change in our world through the hearts of men over which Franz Alt enthuses will never happen. I state this because I find no real grounds in the previous history of mankind which would justify such a hope. And in this I am not speaking against the Bible, because in it I find no promise of the total transformation of our world of experience. The promises of blessedness in the Sermon on the Mount are precisely not concerned with this world of ours, whose outstanding feature is that it must be shaped on the responsibility of human beings themselves.[26]

Assessing our chances of establishing peace, he comes to the following conclusion:

Basically then, it is we who redeem ourselves by imitating the Master and fulfilling his commands. But I do not believe that in His commands Jesus intended to convince us of the futility of grace.[27]

And he states further:

Franz Alt's references to the Sermon on the Mount do not convince me, because nowhere in the Bible do I find the Utopia of a society of purely good hearts before the dissolution of our history.[28]

Bahá'ís, on the other hand, recognise neither a 'society of purely good hearts' nor the 'dissolution of our history'. Is one really untrue to Christ if one regards 'peace on earth' as possible and strives for it, heart and soul, under divine guidance? Certainly the spiritual is a mirror of the material. In the scientific area we have made enormous progress in the past two centuries and still have undreamed-of progress ahead of us. Why should no parallels be conceivable in the intellectual and religious area? Divine mercy is certainly not one-dimensional. Over and above the redemption of the individual, it desires the pacification and redemption of all mankind – especially at an hour when the continued existence of mankind is at risk. But if we human beings were and had to remain as unalterable as our history shows and the critics of the peace movements declare, would we have any moral claim to survival at all? The little regard in which man, the 'crown of creation', is held is expressed in the following words:

Any analogies drawn from observations in the animal world, showing that the weaker or more defenceless are not attacked, are, as human history amply demonstrates, not reliable.[29]

Why should it always be possible to move mountains by faith on the individual level but never on the social and political level? And if man is the image of God, then why is mankind not? Is it not presumptuous to regard God's mercy as possible only within specific bounds? At a time when materialism and nihilism have the upper hand, it is easy to forget what the Divine Manifestations have achieved as teachers of mankind. For instance, it is scarcely possible to calculate how much good Christians have done over the centuries and will do again for Christ's sake. But why should Christ have set the touchstone 'By their fruits shall ye know them', if in his very essence man were quite unable to change and those fruits were only of a superficial nature? The fact that man always, in all circumstances, both here and in the hereafter, is dependent on God's grace is a subject in itself, and one that is supported by all religions.

This is expressed very vividly in the short obligatory prayer of the Bahá'ís:

I bear witness, O my God, that Thou hast created me to know Thee and to worship Thee. I testify, at this moment, to my powerlessness and to Thy might, to my poverty and to Thy wealth.

There is none other God but Thee, the Help in Peril, the Self-Subsisting.[30]

However, this absolute dependence of the creature on the creator can in no way justify our inability to make spiritual and intellectual progress towards the 'peace of substance' or 'Most Great Peace', as Bahá'u'lláh has called it. Man will never reach the stage of absolute perfection, nor will there ever be absolutely pure iron or an absolutely pure diamond. Nevertheless, the possibilities of human progress through divine grace are immeasurable. However noble and holy we believe man to be, he can further hallow and ennoble himself. This does not apply only to the individual, it also applies to society, together with its social and political structure. If this were not so it would be presumptuous to speak of a new creation, which, after all, has been and will be the goal and fruit of every religion.

For Bahá'ís there is no problem of self-redemption. Under Bahá'u'lláh's guidance every Bahá'í strives with mind and soul to realise His plan for peace and it is certain that this is possible, indeed willed by God. In this sense the Bahá'í's service to his fellowmen and to the unification of nations is also the service of God.

To speak of heavenly conditions in connection with peace may be misunderstood. Normally, if one talks about heaven something static is implied, certainly nothing dynamic. But peace, that fruit of the unity of mankind, that fruit of justice,[31] is simply harmony between the cells and limbs of the body of humanity, which have of their own free will submitted themselves to a common soul – the Word of God – but with tremendous vitality and a delight in both spiritual and cultural exchange.

In the peace debate centred on religious criteria the principal features are abhorrence of nuclear war and a stand against continuing armament and in favour of disarmament. However, it is not clear what image of man is taken as a basis, with what consequences for the future of humanity. Hence the question: can mankind hope to achieve peace on this earth of ours – yes or no?

Floyd W. Matson explains the implications and consequences of a positive or negative answer:

If it is true, in general, that 'ideas have consequences', then man's ideas about man have the most far-reaching consequences of all. Upon them may depend the structure of government, the patterns of culture, the purpose of education, the design of the future and human or inhuman uses of human beings.[32]

Are we complex machines, or higher animals, eking out an existence in this vale of tears under the compulsion to sin, without hope of peace in the here and now?

Or are we educable beings and capable, as the image of God, of moving mountains and building the kingdom of God on earth?

Bahá'u'lláh reveals:

Would that ye had the power to perceive the things your Lord, the All-Merciful, doth see – things that attest the excellence of your rank, that bear witness to the greatness of your worth, that proclaim the sublimity of your station. God grant that your desires and unmortified passions may not hinder you from that which hath been ordained for you.[33]

Like Christians with the doctrine of original sin, orthodox Jews have their dilemma over the State of Israel. They do not recognise it, because the existence of the State of Israel assumes that the Promised One has already appeared. The Old Testament postulates a parallel between the foundation of the State of Israel and the coming of the Promised One. If the State is founded under the pressure of historical necessity, one would think that Jews in their thousands were wondering whether the Promised One may not in fact have appeared (this naturally applies equally to Christians). But they prefer to dispute the fact that this is the real State, and that the people of Israel really have returned to Palestine.

Even the kingdom of peace of the New Testament: 'Thy kingdom come, Thy will be done on earth as it is in heaven,' assumes the return of the Lord; it would be unthinkable for Christ to teach His people to pray for something that would never happen. Today there is agreement on all sides that we are moving towards alternative extremes: peace or downfall. But in this unique constellation Christians do not ask themselves the obvious question: what is the real position as regards the coming of the promised Prince of Peace? According to the logic of history in terms of salvation, must he not have appeared long since?

To put it still more radically: in order to liberate some Israelite tribes from Egyptian captivity it was necessary for God to send them a Messenger in the person of

Moses. Is it not necessary to the pacification of all humanity and its salvation from total destruction that God should send a Messenger, the Prince of Peace promised and expected in all revealed religions, in order to show us the way out of the impasse of our times?

Theology is Inadequate to the Task

Every theology has its special weaknesses, especially when it encounters a new revelation. Generally unaware of this, the theologians consciously or unconsciously assume that the new Word of God is based on the theology developed by them. To put it another way, they believe that they possess a yardstick against which they can measure the Promised One. In fact, however, the new Messengers of God have always come otherwise than expected in order to liberate religion from human falsification and to proclaim something in the future.

After Bahá'u'lláh had set new criteria in the middle of the last century, the theologians of the religions and churches, without being aware of it, achieved a certain development in this direction. Perhaps I can support this with an example: in the mid-19th century the theologians of the various religions and denominations were entangled in claims to conclusiveness and incomparability. There was a sharp division: faithful here, heathens there; truth here, in its absolute, ultimate flowering, the false prophets and the misguided there. That was the attitude of Jewish theologians to Christianity, of Christian theologians to Islam, not to speak of the extra-Biblical religions. Even Muslims, who according to Muhammad should be tolerant of the people of the Book, that is the Jews and Christians, widely declared them to be unbelievers. In Persia in the last century, for instance, Jews and Christians did not venture into the streets on rainy days because of the danger that Muslim believers might be made unclean by a wet contact, for which there was a severe penalty.

It was in that period that Bahá'u'lláh appeared, teaching the unity of religions, the essential unity of the Revealers and their spiritual identity. He taught that every Messenger of God is the fulfilment and return of the preceding one. Naturally Jewish, Christian and Islamic theologies were at that time unable to accept this truth, which was regarded as a terrible provocation.

Today, however, it is almost as if a cosmic wind had breathed ecumenism, not only into the denominations but also into the religions themselves. In many cases people are no longer so completely convinced that their own position is the only true one, nor can they any longer believe that the other religions are so completely false. A host of theologians in all camps is concerned to develop a principle of both/and, in order to escape this dilemma, but as long as the theologians refuse to recognise without reservation the *unity of religions* and the *unity of God's Messengers*, they will live from hand to mouth and ecumenism will be forced to remain fragmentary.

On the attitude of the Bahá'ís to ecumenism, *World Order*, a Bahá'í magazine in the USA, wrote in 1976:

Is Ecumenism Hopeless?

Ecumenism is out of fashion. Only a few years ago the press regularly reported dozens of meetings, symposia, and conferences at which scholars, clergy, and concerned laymen debated issues raised by the prospect of growing religious unity. No longer. Other interests have crowded ecumenism off the front pages and out of the popular mind. The word itself is gradually resuming the arcane ring it had nearly lost.

The proponents of ecumenism had set themselves a most difficult task. If the reconciliation of Christian sects proved beyond reach, the gap between major religions was too wide to bridge even in theory, even in dreams. Thus the movement lost momentum and was abandoned by many of its supporters. Yet its achievements were not negligible. The idea of religious unity was given currency. Sectarian exclusiveness and claims to a monopoly of truth were vigorously challenged. There developed a healthy desire to know and a capacity to appreciate spiritual traditions other than one's own.

We Bahá'ís feel that the setbacks recently suffered by ecumenism are temporary. We firmly believe in the unity of religions. Seen from the vantage provided by the principle of progressive revelation, Judaism, Christianity, and Islám lose the appearance of incompatibility. A simple reinterpretation of a few key concepts permits us to find the underlying unity and not be misled by assertions of irreconcilable contradictions. At a still deeper level we perceive Hinduism, Buddhism, and Zoroastrianism as members of the same great family, merging into a single religious experience of mankind.

It is, therefore, natural that we should wish ecumenism well and hope that it will regain its vigor. For it represents a right path, a long step in the right direction, that of the unity of religions and of mankind.[34]

Another example of the change in theological attitudes in two successive centuries is the dualism fostered by mid-19th-century theologians of all religions: God here, Satan there. It was not only that people were convinced of the existence of the Devil; all kinds of measures and regulations had been developed in the encounter with him. Exorcism was an ingredient of everyday life; Satanology was accounted a science.

It was at this time that Bahá'u'lláh announced the redemptive principle, actually present in embryonic form in all previous religions, of the *non-existence of absolute evil*.

Nowadays we are at liberty to experience the effect of God's creative Word in our everyday life. Satan and the Devil in their former sense have been displaced from our vocabulary and exorcism evokes in us little more than a puzzled headshake. Christianity has retained only a qualified doctrine of original sin, which is constantly becoming still more qualified and no longer supplies any kind of proof of the existence of an evil principle, or of absolute evil; it is simply a justification of the claim to uniqueness of Christ's revelation.

'Abdu'l-Bahá explains the non-existence of evil as follows:

Error is lack of guidance; darkness is absence of light; ignorance is lack of knowledge; falsehood is lack of truthfulness; blindness is lack of sight; and deafness is lack of hearing. Therefore, error, blindness, deafness and ignorance are non-existent things.[35]

The 'Unsealing of the Wine' by the One who is to come means new spiritual and religious truths, always present in embryo, but not perceived. The fundamental unity of religions is one of 'the hidden things of darkness'[36] that will be brought to light, 'the wisdom of God . . . even the hidden wisdom . . . revealed unto us by . . . the Spirit of God'.[37]

Bahá'u'lláh says:

Contemplate with thine inward eye the chain of successive Revelations that hath linked the Manifestation of Adam with that of the Báb. I testify before God that each one of these Manifestations hath been sent down by the operation of the Divine Will and Purpose, that each hath been the bearer of a specific Message, that each hath been entrusted with a divinely-revealed Book and been commissioned to unravel the mysteries of a mighty Tablet. The measure of the Revelation with which every one of them hath been identified had been definitely fore-ordained.[38]

We should detach ourselves from the past. We must bring our minds and hearts, that is, our whole being, into a new order. It is not enough to love and help our neighbours, and do charitable works; we must be involved in all aspects of a universal divine order.

THREE

We are All in the Same Boat

The Way to Peace is Controversial

A peculiar phenomenon of our age is the emergence of peace movements all over the world. The debate on the achievement and maintenance of peace has become an existential requirement to many.

All over the Western world there is a confrontation between the proponents of armament and their opponents, generally known as the peace movement. Although the two sides represent diametrically opposite standpoints, each firmly believes itself to be in possession of the better, more successful method of achieving and maintaining peace.

Three points have struck me in this hard-fought and undoubtedly long-term debate.

Firstly, the argument has reached a kind of stalemate. Many initial supporters of armament have become uncertain after intensive study of the arguments of the peace movement. Conversely, many once ardent supporters of the peace movement wavered after being confronted over a long period with the massive arguments of the other side.

Secondly, the quality of the two sides' arguments is very variable. Each side's criticism of the other is compelling, while the justification of its own way reveals serious defects. The arguments proposed by the supporters of armament seem to me thin and weak. How in fact can one credibly demonstrate that continued armament is *certain* to result in a peace settlement in the medium or long-term?

But when the supporters of armament criticise the other party's chances of success, their arguments are very strong and convincing. The supporters of armament say: in the past history of nations, those who have shown weakness have been conquered. We are not now in a position to sit down at the same table with our opponents in order to agree on common arms limitation. Each side believes it has to catch up in one area or another of this complicated field of armaments. How can we be sure that our moratorium will automatically cause our opponents to hold back?

The arguments of the peace movement reveal similar weaknesses. Their criticism of the other side is brilliant. In a world grown small, as Alt rightly states, we have a twenty-fold overkill capacity. Figuratively speaking, we now possess 1.6 million Hiroshima bombs, that is 3,300 Hiroshima bombs for London and 60 for Oxford. What is the point of producing a thousand-fold overkill in the name of peace, so that there will soon be a Hiroshima bomb in reserve for every greybeard and every baby? When and how, ask the members of the peace movement, is there to be an end to this madness?

But when the peace movement tries to argue in favour of its own methods, the brilliance is missing. Its spokesmen begin to stammer, because no one can ever know in advance exactly whether his own restraint will be honoured or abused by his opponent. This state of affairs – weak arguments for one's own cause and strong arguments against one's political opponent – has led in practice to a fantastic displacement process over peace matters in the politics of the day. People shift the responsibility for the lack of peace on to the politicians and the politicians on to their colleagues in the other camp.

Thirdly, although both sides – supporters and opponents of armament – proceed under the banners of diametrically opposed methods for the achievement of peace, both cherish a certain basic optimism as regards the conduct of the enemy: the peace movement builds its argument on the fact that non-armament will be honoured by an intelligent opponent as a basis for subsequent agreements on the pacification of the world. The supporters of armament say: we are in a predicament and we must arm, but we have good reason to believe that our opponents will soon indicate their readiness to negotiate and will cease to arm, in order to bring this disastrous development to an end; in other words, an optimistic assessment of the opponent, born of necessity.

Now whether realisation will dawn on one or other of the groups I cannot say, but without optimism as to the basically peaceable attitude of the opposing regime, there can obviously be no peace. We are not all in the same boat simply in the sense that we shall sink or swim together, but also in the sense that we regard all the passengers as willing partners in peace and must take them seriously in order to arrive safely at our destination. Günther Anders has got it absolutely right: 'Either there is peacetime or there is no time at all. Time and peacetime have become identical.'[1]

But if we are really to take seriously the image of the boat, with the nations, religions and races confined within it as partners in peace, we shall have no further difficulty in understanding Bahá'u'lláh when he speaks of the necessity of establishing the *unity of mankind* and teaches us that *peace is the fruit of that unity*.

Peace, the Fruit of Unity

Never again, never again in the history of mankind can we allow ourselves a real war, employing all the means available. So we must reach an understanding with our peace-partners in the boat and remove the causes of war.

The wars of the past were typically waged on behalf of so-called national, racial, religious, political and, last but not least, economic interests. In their own interests, the powerful stirred up the prejudices of the powerless, who were driven into these wars. If our goal is a peaceful, *united world community*, we can locate prejudices as the essential causes of war: racial prejudices, national and religious prejudices, prejudices in the economic sphere, aimed consciously or unconsciously at wealth and independence for their own countries and economic dependence and weakness for the rest.

Many people, millions of soldiers, were brought up in the past and also, unfortunately, in many countries today, in such a way that for these idols they willingly sacrificed their lives, not to speak of slaughtering the enemy.

The world is our common home. We and our partners in peace must make an educational and conscious leap *from the national state to the world state*. Humanity has made such leaps in the past, attempting and realising, one by one, over the millennia *the unity of the family*, of the *clan*, of the *people* and of the *nation*. There is no reason why world unity should not also be achieved, especially when our survival depends on it

The example of the United States of America proves that this is not an eccentric idea. People of various nationalities and races, from Europe, Asia and Africa, emigrated voluntarily or under compulsion to America and today, despite – or perhaps because of – this extraordinary mixture, they are a strong nation. Then why should those who stayed at home, those parts of the individual nations which did not emigrate to the United States, never be able to achieve unity?

There is a force which exerts a more powerful influence on the human soul than any prejudice: the pure spirit of religious truth. In this force lies the solution of mankind's problems. Parallel to the political development from the *unity of the family* to the *unity of all mankind* on the planet, we human beings have undergone a development of consciousness and a religious evolution.

The Emergence of World Consciousness

In the study of the history of civilisation there is what might be called 'the theory of cultural evolution'. In the course of man's general evolution, it is argued, we have seen his archaic consciousness replaced or supplemented and expanded by a 'magical consciousness' and then in turn by a 'mythical consciousness'. Later, through an 'intellectual consciousness' we appropriated a wealth of scientific knowledge and technology. Now we are in the process of developing an 'integral consciousness', a world consciousness indispensable to the existence of a world civilisation and a world culture.[2]

Basically, the existence of the peace movements throughout the world is a sign of the approaching 'integral consciousness'. The motive of these movements is not simply fear of total destruction; to many peace has become an existential need for which some are even prepared to give their lives. In this context it is immaterial whether the methods and proposals offered lead to the goal.

In general, ideas about human behaviour in the community are summed up in two theories:

a. The stimulation theory, based on an image of man which requires reward and punishment in order to adopt social norms;

b. The perfection theory, based on the human being who has his own motivation and his own innate or inculcated moral values and behaves accordingly.

Both theories are considered in the Bahá'í scriptures. The following words of Bahá'u'lláh show clearly the supreme significance accorded to reward and punishment even in the new age:

The structure of world stability and order hath been reared upon, and will continue to be sustained by, the twin pillars of reward and punishment.[3]

Even the 'formal peace' which Bahá'u'lláh calls the 'Lesser Peace', must be based on the solidarity of nations, in which any possible aggressor must expect to be punished by all the other nations.

The 'perfection' theory also finds its counterpart: through Bahá'í education and the blessings of the 'Lesser Peace', humanity in the course of the centuries will increasingly share in the 'Most Great Peace' which is the true goal and fruit of the Bahá'í revelation. This 'peace of substance' is described by the founder of the Bahá'í Faith in the following words:

If any man were to meditate on that which the Scriptures, sent down from the heaven of God's holy Will, have revealed, he will readily recognise that their purpose is that all men shall be regarded as one soul, so that the seal bearing the words 'The Kingdom shall be God's' may be stamped on every heart, and the light of Divine bounty, of grace, and mercy may envelop all mankind. The one true God, exalted be His glory, hath wished nothing for Himself. The allegiance of mankind profiteth Him not, neither doth its perversity harm Him. The Bird of the Realm of Utterance voiceth continually this call: 'All things have I willed for thee, and thee, too, for thine own sake.'[4]

O well-beloved ones! The tabernacle of unity hath been raised; regard ye not one another as strangers. Ye are the fruits of one tree and the leaves of one branch.[5]

The Evolution of Religion in History

In the religious sphere we can start with so-called archaic and primitive cultures. Later we can observe the dawning of the light of religion in the nascent tribes – there are still tribal religions in various parts of the world – and then in the foundation of national, or *people's religions*; as Judaism originally was. Only later came the *high religions*, which now essentially determine the religious picture of the world. Common to religions is the proclamation of the coming or return of a revealer 'in the fullness of time'. His task is to bring peace on earth in righteousness. At the same time this Prince of Peace rings in the age of world religion in which God will be the shepherd and the whole of humanity a single flock.

Bahá'u'lláh, founder of the Bahá'í Faith, lays claim to
being the Promised One of all religions and the Prince of
Peace. Through Him, through his teachings and the
world order that bears His name, we receive the
necessary psychological equipment for peace, the qualifi-
cations for leading life in conformity with a goal as well
as an administrative order for the realisation of peace.

Even many religious people have no hope of seeing a
way out of the impasse in our time through divine help.
They reject untested the idea that Bahá'u'lláh might be
the promised Prince of Peace.

It is often asserted in all seriousness that the greatest
work in human history, the establishment of peace, is a
matter for the politicians alone.

The more recent peace movements aim directly at
political solutions, in the belief that peace can be attained
only through pressure on the politicians; but peace can
endure only by uniting in a just world order.

The Stage of Maturity

The new world order must do justice to one particular
element: the maturity of the peace-partners in our
common boat.

There are two possibilities, extreme and dramatic,
whether negative or positive, as regards the fate of the
boat's occupants, our fate. If negative, the boat will
finally sink: mankind and its civilisation will commit
suicide. If positive, the occupants of the boat, as often
happens in life, may possibly undergo a sudden process
of maturing in the harshness of their common fate; in a
short space they may achieve that 'integral consciousness' and reach the stage of maturity. This means that the

occupants of the boat would never again regard each other as strangers.

The consequences of this state of maturity are manifold and wonderful. Attentive study of the sayings of the ancient prophets on the Kingdom of Peace which is now well within our reach, discloses that they fall into ecstasy in their description of that time, almost unable to find the words to describe its gloriousness. That time is referred to as the *Day of God*, a superlative which allows of no further intensification.

Sceptics may object: 'All very fine of course, but I can't imagine this Bahá'í vision taking shape.' We are warned not to go chasing off after Utopia.

But what is Utopia?

Many things that subsequently took shape were long regarded as Utopian. As Franz Alt quite rightly says:

> Those who spoke a hundred years ago of ending child labour, or three hundred years ago of overcoming slavery, or who claimed five hundred years ago that the earth turns round the sun, and those who said eight hundred years ago that plague could be conquered, were laughed to scorn.[6]

Through the ages, child labour, slavery, geocentrism and plague were accepted by the mass of humanity as inevitable. Only a few dreamers and Utopians fought against these contradictions in community life – and eventually emerged victorious. Why should it be otherwise with peace on earth, the central question of our common existence? It is man's chance of survival that seems Utopian, unless he can achieve unity.

The Steps towards Peace are Obvious

The goal of peace on earth is part of the divine plan of salvation. The prophets of the past perceived this goal and Bahá'u'lláh has shown the way. He has revealed what structures mankind must accept to make peace possible on earth. Peace on earth is no illusory Utopia.

The leap from the grim world of today to the Kingdom of Peace and a just world order is so great that it overtaxes our imagination. But if we divide the transition to peace into a number of small steps we can see that each individual one is not only possible, but often quite obvious.

Above all, each is no more than could reasonably be expected of those concerned at the time.

Here are some examples:

— Is it realistic or Utopian that in the next few years the great powers should actually reach agreement on disarmament, either voluntarily or following a world-wide shock?

— Is it realistic or Utopian that under an international agreement rich countries should become sponsors to poor countries and encourage their development more intensively than before?

— Is it realistic or Utopian that women should acquire more rights, so that in the near future equality becomes a reality, everywhere, not only in a few industrialised countries?

— Is it realistic or Utopian that the scientists of the world should work together? It is becoming increasingly difficult to maintain secrecy in science and technology. For instance, sixteen-year-old schoolboys succeeded in cracking a secret code of the Pentagon computer. Can

sciences and technologies possibly be divided into
'Western' and 'Eastern' in the age of satellites and
computers?
– Is it realistic or Utopian that our children should
receive integrated moral and political teaching at an early
age? For instance, on how elections will be held in a
society permeated with spirituality, and what genuine
consultation means?[7] From the worst dictatorial regimes
of past millennia, have we not progressed in many
countries to democratic forms of government worthier
of man? Why should progress end here?

Jonathan Schell writes: 'If it is "utopian" to want to
survive, then it must be "realistic" to wish to be dead.'[8]
The gulf between the positions of the peace movement
and its critics can be bridged if we admit that we have
entered into a new era. One pointer is the fact that today
for the first time in human history, peace has become an
existential requirement to many people (and I do not
mean only Bahá'ís). Young people, above all, have
become the champions of peace in many countries,
prepared to make great sacrifices in its name. What
moves them is more than fear of catastrophe, and it
would be wrong to accuse them of irrational fervour.

The needs of the moment are so great that even to
alleviate them will require all the forces of peace-loving
people. Biafra the day before yesterday, Vietnam
yesterday and Ethiopia today, to mention only a few
focal points of suffering. Bahá'ís may be reproached for
not doing enough for the disadvantaged, but the truth is
that the opportunities and powers of the Bahá'ís are
limited by their relatively small numbers. After all, their
religion was founded only 140 years ago, and in some

countries they are also being persecuted. For the short-term needs of the world their contributions are mere drops on hot stone. Nevertheless, both as individuals and as a community Bahá'ís are solidly behind all the organisations which provide aid for suffering humanity, in every possible area. They help and support such projects on individual, local, national and international levels.

But to Bahá'ís, Bahá'u'lláh's real task for them is to work as the 'leaven' of peace. On closer investigation one sees that Bahá'ís are conscientiously laying the foundations of an international peace movement, a movement incorporating many of the best current proposals for peace: educational initiatives; developing new ways of thinking, necessary to a world without war; building models for a new political order that will link the peoples of the world in a network of peace. Bahá'í methods offer a new way of decision-making, to which propaganda, manipulation and the power struggle are alien. A new consciousness and far-reaching emotional ties are being created; intercultural exchange in all areas is demanded and encouraged. But above all, faith offers what the war-burdened world most needs: the spiritual strength to alter the collective consciousness of mankind in such a way that war will for ever be impossible and will no longer represent a category of political thought and action.

For a Brahman in India, this new insight may mean that the lower castes are equally his brothers and sisters; for an African it may mean accepting the members of a neighbouring tribe without prejudice; for a man from the Middle East it may mean developing a new understanding for the rights of women. For a European or American, new hope may dawn of the possibility of peace, peace without and within. Here the racial question and the evolution of a just social order offer a broad field of action. For the believer it may mean a new understanding of other religions, whereas an atheist or humanist will have to ask himself if the Bahá'í Faith does not embody many of his ideals. In fact it is sometimes difficult for an outsider to judge whether the Bahá'í Faith is more a religion or a peace movement, since most of the doctrines of the Faith revolve around the aim of peace. It is increasingly recognised that a genuine peace movement must be radical: must grasp everything by the roots.

Unity, an Existential Need

The Bahá'í Faith is the religion of peace, the religion of unity. Peace is not only to be defined in cognitive terms: it has a strong existential component. We must allow ourselves to be re-educated for peace in personal experience and understanding, to absorb Bahá'u'lláh's vision and make it our life's purpose. Academic discussions will not do; we must also realise that for the *oneness of humanity* (naturally in the sense of *unity in diversity*, not of *uniformity*) a strong emotional component is necessary.

The Germans, to take one example, know with their reason that a Jew is their equal, but since no far-reaching emotional unification has taken place through a profound spiritual and religious impulse, the old historical gulfs remain to some extent, only awaiting an opportunity or a demagogue to reveal themselves openly.

When my grandfather became a Bahá'í, identifying himself both emotionally and existentially with the teaching of Bahá'u'lláh about the unity of mankind, he often spoke of his wish and hope that through marriage his descendants might embrace every possible religion. He was blessed with many descendants: on the distaff side alone, the family produced 12 children, 40 grandchildren and more than 100 great-grandchildren, with their partners. Our extended family now includes former Muslims, former Catholics and Protestants, former Jews and Hindus and even former Zoroastrians. All we lack are former Buddhists. The extended family comprises more than 24 nationalities, from all five continents. Thanks to the education we owe to our faith, many apparently insuperable barriers are simply non-existent for us.

FOUR

World Order, A Necessity

Human Rights in a Disrupted World

The Declaration of Human Rights by the United Nations was a milestone of progress in the history of mankind. Nevertheless, if we ask ourselves about the practical significance of this declaration in the life of the peoples of the world, the results are depressing.

Here are some examples: since the Second World War, between 40 and 60 million people have died in regional wars, not including people killed by state and private terrorism. If one then considers the millions dead of hunger or disease who could have been assisted by international aid, the figure is at least double. The number of those imprisoned, tortured and abducted is simply enormous. The world witnessed the killing of half the population of a country such as Cambodia. Some rulers were able to slaughter thousands of people and even whole tribes over the years with impunity. If we can believe the statements of Amnesty International, the international situation today is worse than ever before. The whole of mankind is concerned, as never before in history, over every one of these injustices, every massacre. Help is given here and there, but mankind as a whole is forced to look on in horror at torture and atrocities without being able to act effectively against them.

This is because the realisation of human rights has to be based on a *world order*, which we do not yet possess. Mankind is like a body: if one limb is diseased, the other organs with their various functions must be able to rush to its aid and fight the disease. By blood transfusions and the enrichment of white corpuscles a cure is attempted, and the body even exploits fever to heal the diseased limb. For want of a world order, we are all impotent observers with a bad conscience.

Humanity stands at the crossroads. According to many cultural historians, the question whether the human species is to be or not to be will be answered in our generation. I mention this well-known fact to show that world problems must not be reduced to the level of the nuclear armament of the great powers. It would be very welcome if the great powers concluded binding agreements on arms limitation, but that is not enough to achieve peace.

An Overall Solution is Necessary

If in general I compare the positions taken up in the peace debate with mine as a Bahá'í, I note that most are concerned with *minimal* demands, whereas Bahá'ís, following Bahá'u'lláh, wrap all the requirements for the pacification of the world as it were in one package and identify themselves totally with it. It might be thought that a single step, a partial aspect of world peace, would be easier to attain than the whole, all at once. That is not my view. Fear, need and last-minute panic are poor counsellors. What mankind needs is a total solution in a single mould, an architectural model which may be implemented gradually. Such a solution can come solely from a divine source, not only because such a concept transcends the conditional, limited horizon of our great minds, but also because the Divine Revealer must first educate, or more precisely create the people to live peacefully together in a united world. Bahá'u'lláh himself says:

Is it within human power . . . to effect in the constituent elements of any of the minute and indivisible particles of matter so complete a transformation as to transmute it into purest gold? Perplexing and difficult as this may appear, the still greater task of converting satanic strength into heavenly power is one that We have been empowered to accomplish . . . The Word of God, alone, can claim the distinction of being endowed with the capacity required for so great and far-reaching a change.[1]

Our best thinkers, authors and peace researchers are only now on the trail. In their findings I can see nothing which Bahá'u'lláh had not already considered 120 years ago in His great and at the same time extremely simple plan.

In the peace debate of recent years the works of Jonathan Schell and Günther Anders deserve special attention. Both rightly assert that with the splitting of the atom and the manufacture of the nuclear bomb we have entered into a new age of human history. Knowledge of the atom and the bomb can never again be extinguished. If all the nuclear bombs in the world were to be simultaneously destroyed today, the problem would by no means be solved, because an interested power could produce a fresh arsenal of them in a few months. Even the destruction of nuclear laboratories, machines and apparatus would not be a solution; they too could be reproduced in quite a short time.

We are now confronted for the first time with a *second death*, the death of mankind. Still more perilous than the direct effects of the innumerable nuclear bombs, the use of which would lead to indescribable destruction, would be the *destruction of the biosphere*, jeopardising the habitability of the earth. There is disagreement as to whether Günther Anders or Jonathan Schell was the first to formulate this and similar ideas.[2]

I would quote Bahá'u'lláh (1817–92) and leave the reader to judge. In about 1873 Bahá'u'lláh wrote in the 'Words of Paradise':

In all matters moderation is desirable. If a thing is carried to excess, it will prove a source of evil. Consider the civilization of the West, how it hath agitated and alarmed the peoples of the world. An infernal engine hath been devised, and hath proved so cruel a weapon of destruction that its like none hath ever witnessed or heard. The purging of such deeply-rooted and overwhelming corruptions cannot be effected unless the peoples of the world unite in pursuit of one common aim and embrace one universal faith. Incline your ears unto the Call of this Wronged One and adhere firmly to the Lesser Peace.

Strange and astonishing things exist in the earth but they are hidden from the minds and the understanding of men. These things are capable of changing the whole atmosphere of the earth and their contamination would prove lethal.[3]

Examining the ecological dangers, only hints of which are now with us, Bahá'u'lláh writes:

The civilization, so often vaunted by the learned exponents of arts and sciences, will, if allowed to overleap the bounds of moderation, bring great evil upon men. Thus warneth you He Who is the All-Knowing. If carried to excess, civilization will prove as prolific a source of evil as it had been of goodness when kept within the restraints of moderation. Meditate on this, O people, and be not of them that wander distraught in the wilderness of error. The day is approaching when its flame will devour the cities, when the Tongue of Grandeur will proclaim: 'The Kingdom is God's, the Almighty, the All-Praised!'[4]

He turns to the rulers of the time and describes the new impotence of the mighty in the face of the armament spiral:

Compose your differences, and reduce your armaments, that the burden of your expenditures may be lightened, and that your minds and hearts may be tranquillized. Heal the dissensions that divide you, and ye will no longer be in need of any armaments except what the protection of your cities and territories demandeth. Fear ye God, and take heed not to outstrip the bounds of moderation, and be numbered among the extravagant.

We have learned that you are increasing your outlay every year, and are laying the burden thereof on your subjects. This, verily, is more than they can bear, and is a grievous injustice . . .

If ye pay no heed unto the counsels which, in peerless and unequivocal language, We have revealed in this Tablet, Divine chastisement shall assail you from every direction, and the sentence of his justice shall be pronounced against you. On that day ye shall have no power to resist Him, and shall recognize your own impotence. Have mercy on yourselves and on those beneath you.[5]

National Sovereignty: A Fetish

We have reached a dead end in the special-interest politics of the sovereign national state. It is *here* that the way out must begin.

Werner Becker, Professor of Philosophy at the University of Frankfurt, has reservations with regard to the possibility of friendship between peoples and nations. He writes:

In the relationship between nations the positive and intense feelings which must prevail in order to make and maintain friendship between human beings do not exist. Of course we know people who insist that they love the French, the British, the Americans or the Italians. But it makes little sense to claim that whole nations have friendly feelings towards each other. Even an individual who says he 'loves' the French, the British or the Americans, has to admit that he is using this highly emotional word in a different sense from when he speaks of love or friendship between two people. Normally, where friendly relations between states are concerned, it would be more accurate to describe them as cupboard love.[6]

Could not these arguments have been adduced only a few generations ago regarding relations among the American colonies? And yet these regions have united within the United States of America just as the nations must unite in a world federation! To show that there is no alternative let us look at a working hypothesis which is highly likely to materialise: if the basically immoral strategy of deterrence suddenly fails, what then?

What will happen after the collapse of a poker game played with increasingly high stakes? What happens next, when the catastrophe is here but not everybody has been wiped out? Will there then be a new version of the strategy of deterrence among the remaining nations, or, in the melting-pot of suffering, will they unite in a federal world?

The words of Bahá'u'lláh, revealed four generations ago, are a warning to a world which refuses voluntarily to accept His divine gift, the spiritual unity of mankind:

The world is in travail, and its agitation waxeth day by day. Its face is turned towards waywardness and unbelief. Such shall be its plight, that to disclose it now would not be meet and seemly. Its perversity will long continue. And when the appointed hour is come, there shall suddenly appear that which shall cause the limbs of mankind to quake. Then, and only then, will the Divine Standard be unfurled, and the Nightingale of Paradise warble its melody.[7]

The day is approaching when We will have rolled up the world and all that is therein, and spread out a new order in its stead. He, verily, is powerful over all things.[8]

In a world grown small, 150 sovereign states are an unparalleled absurdity which, alas, is accepted fatalistically. Peter Mühlschlegel writes:

Why, despite all the crises and catastrophes, despite the threat of total ruin, do people find it so difficult to take the next, urgently necessary philosophical step along the political road? Why can the peace movement find nothing better to oppose the whole armaments mania, the absurd concept of mutual deterrence by nuclear powers large and small, than the scarcely less absurd notion that peace is conceivable without the threat or use of force? Are they all really so blind, so devoid of all logical sense of justice and all political imagination, that they do not realise how absurd it is when in our shrunken world more that 150 independent national states each defend their sovereign rights with tooth and claw instead of getting together in a federal world state? . . .

. . . Between the new peace movement, with its revived anarchical ideas, and the traditionalist representatives of sovereign national states with their theory of peace by deterrence, we Bahá'ís will have to walk the narrow middle way whose goal is the expansion of the United Nations into a viable and effective federal world state. We shall have to say with increasing clarity that this is the only possible way to secure the 'Lesser Peace' predicted by Bahá'u'lláh, and accordingly any foreign policy directed towards other goals imperils peace. And we shall have to unmask the attitude of those who defend the so-called sovereignty of the 150 national states as the abnormality described by Shoghi Effendi back in 1936: to wit, fetishism.[9]

Another Bahá'í writer, J. Tyson, in demonstrating that war is 'a regular and inevitable by-product of the nation-state system', concludes:

The price of peace is not billions of dollars for ever more destructive weapons; nor is it a trillion dollars for defenses in space. The price of peace is not acceptance of a policy of 'Mutual Assured Destruction'; nor is it acceptance of a multitude of 'little' wars scattered about various corners of the globe. What mankind desperately needs to learn is that the price of peace is national sovereignty, and not all of its national sovereignty at that. War will continue, at one level or another, until the nations relinquish their lawlessness and learn to become law-abiding citizens in the country of Earth. And the sooner mankind learns how to do this, the better for us all.[10]

It is heartening to note that nowadays this view, proclaimed by Bahá'u'lláh 120 years ago, is increasingly shared by those who are thinking about peace.

Jonathan Schell writes:

Today, no matter how strenuously statesmen may assert the 'sovereign' power of their nations, the fact is that they are all caught in an increasingly fine mesh of global life, in which the survival of each nation depends on the survival of all. There is no 'sovereign' right to destroy the earthly creation on which everyone depends for survival . . . More and more, the earth is coming to resemble a single body.[11]

Human Rights in the Context of World Order

In 1947, when the United Nations formulated the Declaration of Human Rights, the Bahá'í International Community compiled their proposals and submitted them to the advisory board.[12]

Here are some extracts:

The source of human rights is the endowment of qualities, virtues and powers which God has bestowed upon mankind without discrimination of sex, race, creed or nation. To fulfil the possibilities of this divine endowment is the purpose of human existence.

The modern national state came into existence as a unifier of diverse races and peoples. It has been a social truce observed by or enforced upon communities previously separate, independent and hostile. Historically the nation represented a great moral victory, a definite and important stage in human progress. It has raised the condition of the masses of people, substituted constitutional law for the arbitrary authority of the tribe, extended education and knowledge, mitigated the effect of sectarian disputes, and enlarged the social world of the average man. It provided conditions under which natural science could develop, inventions be put into operation, and industrialisation give man mastery over nature.

The national state has reached the limits of its development as an independent, self-directed social body. A world science, a world economy and a world consciousness, riding the wave of a new and universal movement of spiritual evolution, lay the foundations of world order. Conceived of as an end in itself, the national state has come to be a denial of the oneness of mankind, the source of general disruption opposed to the true interests of its people.

The true destiny of the national state is to build the bridge from local autonomy to world unity. It can preserve its moral heritage and function only as it contributes to the establishment of a sovereign world. Both state and people are needed to serve as the strong pillar supporting the new institutions reflecting the full and final expression of human relationships in an ordered society.

World order is nothing else than the administrative aspect of brotherhood, and man's right to social order can not be dissociated from his right to a world faith.

World order has become legally possible, socially imperative, and divinely ordained. The principle of federation has already united previously independent communities diverse in race, language, religion and size of population. The nations can find just expression for their legitimate rights and needs through proportionate representation in a supranational body. Until world citizenship is guaranteed as a social status, the human rights and privileges developed in the past are undermined by the disruption of modern society.

In the shadow of 1984, Orwell Year, 37 or 38 years later, there is nothing to be added to these world-embracing principles.

FIVE

Grappling with a Difficult Heritage

Our Earth – A Small Town

In the various contributions to the debate on peace we constantly hear, from the politicians in particular, that we in the West have achieved a considerable degree of freedom and economic prosperity, values worth defending.

I therefore intend, on the next few pages, to try to present a bird's eye view of our world.

It can scarcely be claimed nowadays that certain industrially developed countries which are economically on the sunny side represent either structurally or morally the healthy world to which the others need only progress. I have many professional connections with the developing countries. Familiarity with the economic and social structure of those countries through constant contact and many journeys leads to a sad sobriety as regards the role of both eastern and western industrial nations in the development of those countries. One becomes immune to catchwords like freedom and democracy, not to mention Christian policies. Many

demands which would be justified at national level begin
to look problematic.

For instance, in my consciousness the demand for more
technological advances translates into the following:

Where one hour of exported work used to be worth 200
kilos of bananas, it is now to be raised to 400 kilos. Do we
still know what hunger is in the West? Do we know that a
fortnight's arms expenditure would wipe out the world's
starvation? The only solution is *to grasp and be aware of the
world as a single unit.*

According to my observations, terms of trade have
altered over the last ten years in many areas, greatly to the
disadvantage of the developing countries. The poor carpet-
maker (income 50p a day, with no welfare back-up, for a
10-hour day and 7 working days a week) has to work five
times as long as ten years ago in many areas in order to buy
the same medicine for his sick child. Often only the name of
slavery has been done away with.

Remember that the twenty countries at the bottom of the
list of sovereign states have less national income,
altogether, than the annual turnover of a single multina-
tional company. In addition to this, the slipstream of the
great nations' interests is so strong that the small ones can
scarcely be more than willing, or at most unruly playthings
in the international field. To find out what a mockery the
much-proclaimed equality of nations really is, one need
only enquire into the conditions for entry visas to the
various countries when submitting a passport from a poor
country.

We still find it difficult to think and feel in worldwide
contexts, in magnitudes of millions of square kilometres
and millions of people. So let us reduce the world to a size
accessible to our experience: our planet with its 4,700

million-odd inhabitants is comparable to a small town with a population of 4,700. There we live and bear responsibility for the town's welfare. We are therefore ashamed to observe, day in, day out, that some catastrophic conditions prevail in this small town.

No less than 2,500 of the 4,700 inhabitants are undernourished or starving. Two out of three inhabitants – mostly those who are also starving – can neither read nor write. Five hundred inhabitants are always sick because there are no doctors, medicines or hygiene for them. On the world scale that is 500 million people, or eight times the population of the United Kingdom.

The 700 people in the northern quarter of the town are well-to-do, because they own the plants and factories in many other parts of the town, or work in the well-developed industrial area. Every employee working in the north earns twenty times as much as each of the remaining 4,000 who live in the poor southern quarter. Often the conditions in the poor quarter are so terrible that one wonders how the rich can go about their business without any conflict of conscience.

But the well-being of the north is also deceptive. Every other adult there admits to feelings of anxiety. Three out of four young people are afraid of everyday life. The doctors claim that the majority of their patients are not at all ill physically, but have mental ailments. Small wonder that many of these unbalanced people take refuge in incessant entertainment, aggression, brutality or vandalism, or join one sect or another of the many on offer. Many people try to solve their problems by escaping to narcotics: alcohol, tobacco, drugs. Large numbers of the inhabitants of the respectable northern quarter of the town have lost a reasonable attitude to work and achievement. Instead of looking for ways to help their fellow citizens in the poor quarter towards work and affluence, they try to organise their own lives without work. Many of the inhabitants of the northern part have lost their relationship with the values that make life worth living. Small wonder that the sensitive young people seek a way out in extreme substitute values and sham ideals. Since the poor are ignorant and the rich indifferent, since the town is badly organised, it has not yet been possible to bring about an improvement in conditions. Moreover, there are also 20 slaves in this town, who are still being bought and sold today.

Every clan in our little town (every nation state in the great world) is primarily concerned with its own well-being, its own safety and its own power. The attitude is 'If you're not for me, you're against me'. Every clan claims that its own relations are in need of protection (protection from aggressors, protection of sovereignty, protection of ideology, protection of living standards, etc.) to justify its armaments. In order to protect itself against other kinship groups, every family, whether rich or poor, spends a large proportion of its income on the purchase of weapons and munitions, so that the town resembles an arsenal. Many rich families have stored enough dynamite to enable them to raze the town to the ground several times over at any moment. But that is not enough for our inhabitants. From fear of each other they acquire more and more effective explosives in order to be able to bring about this possible destruction still more rapidly. Of course there is a Town Council (the United Nations) but it has little authority and little power; it can do nothing against the power-conscious heads of families.

By the end of the twentieth century (failing total destruction) the number of inhabitants of our little town will have grown to 6,100. So if there are now 2,500 suffering from hunger and unable to read and write, there will then be more than 4,000. The poor will become poorer, the rich richer. The number of the sick and disadvantaged will more than double. But the rich too will become unhappier. The lack of ideals that make life worth living will turn the best people into enemies of society and its order.

Even the blessings of modern civilisation to which we owe our high standard of living will – if the search for more and more prosperity continues at the expense of the environment – poison the earth and water and contaminate the air.

It is obvious that our little town needs a new order. Our world, in which everyone has become everyone else's neighbour, needs a new world order.

Neither Eastern nor Western

The history of past millennia to the present day is evidence of the attempts of the individual clans in our town (tribes, peoples, nations) to achieve prosperity, security and peace at the expense of the others.

These attempts have failed again and again; 'war years' have been the rule and 'peace years' rare exceptions in history, yet we still constantly offer our own form of order as a model for the public order (world order) so urgently needed. But the new order cannot proceed from the self-centred orders of individual families (states), because the new order must be *universally* designed to do justice to the needs and the best possible evolution of all the families. This means that the standards on which this order is based must deal with the inhabitants of our little town as a single family (mankind as a unit) and give peace to them as a whole.

What is more, these standards must have the necessary force and impetus to break out of the present selfish 'sub-orders' and contribute whole-heartedly to the cause of order in our town (the order of mankind). We should not underestimate the sacrifices which individual citizens and the community of men of goodwill must make for a period of time, until the new order becomes apparent throughout the town and has withstood the test of practice.

Courage to Begin Afresh

Over the years the people of our little town have grown more critical, more desperate, but also more mature. They recognise that without an immense step forward it will no longer be possible to ensure individual and collective peace, unity and prosperity for all. The old order has grown irretrievably rotten. The forms of order on offer today will not even satisfy the requirements of the town-quarter in which they originated and grew up, much less the requirements of the inhabitants of the whole town, with its enormous multiplicity of historical and cultural ties.

The doctrines and commandments of Bahá'u'lláh for the rehabilitation of our little town are set out below, but it is important to remember that Bahá'u'lláh constantly and emphatically insisted that He spoke under divine authority. It was not He, a man who had never had the chance to go to school and who spent some forty years in prison and exile, who designed the peace plan for our town. It was God who entrusted it to Him. He speaks of himself as a leaf moved by the wind of God's Will.

The Bahá'í Call to Peace

Bahá'u'lláh's peace plan envisages international institutions to legislate for the whole of mankind, to coordinate the interests of nations within the family of nations and to adjudicate in disputes between the nations and implement the judgements.

One hundred and twenty years ago Bahá'u'lláh was already summoning all the nations to worldwide solidarity:

The Great Being, wishing to reveal the prerequisites of the peace and tranquillity of the world and the advancement of its peoples, hath written: The time must come when the imperative necessity for the holding of a vast, an all-embracing assemblage of men will be universally realised. The rulers and kings of the earth must needs attend it, and, participating in its deliberations, must consider such ways and means as will lay the foundations of the world's Great Peace amongst men. Such a peace demandeth that the Great Powers should resolve, for the sake of the tranquillity of the peoples of the earth, to be fully reconciled among themselves. Should any king take up arms against another, all should unitedly arise and prevent him. If this be done, the nations of the world will no longer require any armaments, except for the purpose of preserving the security of their realms and of maintaining internal order within their territories.[1]

Bahá'u'lláh sent out letters to the rulers of the world, challenging them to establish peace on earth. 'These fruitless strifes, these ruinous wars shall pass away, and the "Most Great Peace" shall come', he is reported to have said (see p. 112) – but his message went unheard.

In October 1985 the Universal House of Justice, following the example of Bahá'u'lláh and on the occasion of the opening of the United Nations Peace Year, sent a message addressed 'To the Peoples of the World'. The Bahá'í institutions and individual Bahá'ís are striving to make this message, entitled *The Promise of World Peace*, accessible to the whole of humanity.

Ervin Lazslo, editor-in-chief of the *World Encyclopedia of Peace* and a member of the Club of Rome, writes:

The Bahá'í call for peace comes at a crucial moment in the history of humanity. Peace in the contemporary world is no longer an option but a necessity. All leaders and peoples of the world must come to realize this fact, and achieve the maturity which the Bahá'í Faith foresees for the coming of age of humanity.[2]

Recalling Bahá'u'lláh's words: 'The time must come when the imperative necessity for the holding of a vast, an all-embracing assemblage of men will be universally realised,' the Universal House of Justice comments: 'The holding of this mighty convocation is long overdue.'

'World peace is not only possible but inevitable,' they write. 'The Great Peace towards which people of good will throughout the centuries have inclined their hearts, of which seers and poets for countless generations have expressed their vision, and for which from age to age the sacred scriptures of mankind have constantly held the promise, is now at long last within the reach of the nations.'

But, 'Whether peace is to be reached only after unimaginable horrors precipitated by humanity's stubborn clinging to old patterns of behaviour, or is to be embraced now by an act of consultative will, is the choice before all who inhabit the earth.'[3]

Some Important Principles of the New World Order

'The abolition of war is not simply a matter of signing treaties and protocols,' writes the Universal House of Justice. 'It is a complex task requiring a new level of commitment to resolving issues not customarily associated with the pursuit of peace.'

'. . . The primary question to be resolved is how the present world, with its entrenched pattern of conflict, can change to a world in which harmony and co-operation will prevail.'[4]

'To achieve peace', writes Ervin Lazslo, 'we need a new orientation of thought and a new knowledge of the dynamics of change in the history of human society. Both have been grasped in their essence in the Bahá'í teachings.'[5]

These principles proclaimed by Bahá'u'lláh, now welcomed into many hearts and minds, represent as a whole a further step towards the realisation of world peace.

1. *The key to Bahá'u'lláh's programme is the word 'unity'.*

World order can be founded only on an unshakeable consciousness of the oneness of mankind, . . . the first fundamental prerequisite for reorganization and administration of the world as one country, the home of humankind. Universal acceptance of this spiritual principle is essential to any successful attempt to establish world peace. It should therefore be universally proclaimed, taught in schools, and constantly asserted in every nation as preparation for the organic change in the structure of society which it implies.[6]

The disparity of culture, race, nation and religion must not be ignored. Nevertheless, the interests of the individual groups are best served if the whole of mankind is regarded as an organic whole and the good of all becomes the yardstick of action.

The unity mapped out for us by Bahá'u'lláh is an organic unity, a *unity in diversity*.

2. The widespread national, social, religious or racial *prejudices* which govern minds and spirits *must be discarded*;

for prejudices have always led only to misunderstanding, conflict and hatred.

The Universal House of Justice calls for the 'abandonment of prejudice – prejudice of every kind – race, class, colour, creed, nation, sex, degree of material civilization, everything which enables people to consider themselves superior to others'.[7]

All wars are rooted in prejudice. In the Federal Republic of Germany Badi Panahi carried out and analysed representative surveys and reached the following conclusion:

The forces and factors which inhibit the realisation of the unity of mankind or a single world do not lie in a wilful aggressive drive; they lie in deep-rooted but acquired social prejudices which drag on through the life of the nations like an hereditary disease from generation to generation.[8]

Proceeding from a 'unity of prejudice', Panahi describes the close connection between aggressive attitudes and social stereotypes:

People who, for instance, regard wars as inevitable and express themselves with cynical destructiveness about all efforts to remove them, also resent the view that all human races are of equal value. People who are afraid of the multiplication of 'inferior' races and regard the world as positively unfriendly and threatening also incline towards exaggerated contrasts, especially in distinguishing categories of 'weak' and 'strong'. As regards questions of morality, such types develop a kind of pharisaical self-righteousness. The inclination to project their own unpleasant feelings on to others or to claim a logical purpose for some obscurely motivated action, is a further syndrome of prejudice. As in paranoia, prejudiced people develop manias about other human groups, foreigners and minorities.[9]

According to the yardsticks laid down by Bahá'u'lláh it is

possible for every human being gradually to recognise and disperse the centuries-old conscious and unconscious prejudices. Moreover, the social order founded by Bahá'u'lláh helps to unmask and overcome all kinds of group egoisms. The variety of human beings must be seen as a source of enrichment and progress, not as a justification for self-righteousness and oppression.

Oddly enough, most people regard themselves as ready for peace. Since most of them have little political or social responsibility and are not in the spotlight, they are not subject to trial by public opinion, so that they never doubt their belief in their own readiness for peace. But if one were to take as a yardstick Bahá'u'lláh's commandments, principles and doctrines which are essential to peace, we would soon see that we are still far from ready. More in some cases, less in others, we are an amalgam of socially inherited or acquired prejudices which are merely inflated and channelled by bad politicians. Often enough we are content to condemn such politicians for failing to create a Golden Age from our leaden hearts. That is why every responsible citizen has a duty to test all the standards set by Bahá'u'lláh for the individual and for the entire family of nations by considering whether there are any sensible alternatives.

3. *All religions have a common foundation.*

No serious attempt to set human affairs aright, to achieve world peace, can ignore religion. Man's perception and practice of it are largely the stuff of history. An eminent historian described religion as a 'faculty of human nature'. That the perversion of this faculty has contributed to much of the confusion in society and the conflicts in and between individuals can hardly be denied. But neither can any fair-minded observer discount the preponderating influence exerted by religion on the vital expressions of civilization. Furthermore, its indispensability to social order has repeatedly been demonstrated by its direct effect on laws and morality.

Writing of religion as a social force, Bahá'u'lláh said:'Religion is the greatest of all means for the establishment of order in the world and for the peaceful contentment of all that dwell therein.' Referring to the eclipse or corruption of religion, he wrote: 'Should the lamp of religion be obscured, chaos and confusion will ensue, and the lights of fairness, of justice, of tranquillity and peace cease to shine.'[10]

The *unity of God* taught by all the major religions leads to the recognition of the *unity of God's Messengers*. They draw on the same source and have proclaimed God's Will at different times under different conditions to our world. In its origins the unity of religions obliges us to regard all people, the images of God, as a single unit, regardless of the historical and social barriers which have divided them into many warring groups.

The various religions in the history of mankind should be regarded, then, not as isolated phenomena unconnected with one another but as a chain whose links are welded together. All of them stem from the same divine source and every religion builds on the religion preceding it. Besides the common kernel, the successive religions, corresponding to the needs and development of peoples, demonstrate the progressive structures of order and an increasingly superior legislation. We can therefore speak of the relativity of religious truth and a progressive revelation to mankind. *The unity of religions* means, in turn, that the knowledge of the latest Revealer is the key to admission to the world of faith. The new doctrines and commandments are God's purpose for the peoples of the present, and they have the power to change people and to call new social structures into being.

The question may then arise: if all religions flow from the

same divine source and the Bahá'í Faith knows itself to be
fully linked with the previous Messengers of God –
Abraham, Moses, Zarathustra, Krishna, Jesus, Buddha,
Muhammad – how is it that the Bahá'ís today see the
crystallisation point for the unification of mankind only in
Bahá'u'lláh?

Note, firstly, that religions, like everything that lives,
are subject to a *cyclical development*, which resembles
the cycle of nature's year from spring to winter. Consequently, at the beginning of its evolution every religion has
been able to transmit enormous impulses and permanently
influence the life of the individual and society, even to the
extent of transforming them. Every religion has drawn on
deeper life-springs than could the peoples outside its sphere
of influence. The followers of these new religions could
speak with some justice of a new creation. All God's
Messengers are therefore the actual *educators of mankind*,
who have transmitted to the peoples of the earth the
greatest impulses known to history, each of which has
carried humanity to a new stage of maturity. A fresh
impulse therefore becomes necessary. In addition, these
impulses are subject over time to a loss of momentum, and
it is therefore imperative to turn to the most recent Divine
Dispensation at any one time. This is the fulfilment and
renewal of what has gone before, the guideline and
yardstick of what is present and to come. The doctrines of
Bahá'u'lláh contain all the central truths of the religions of
the past, together with concrete remedies for the ailments
and afflictions of our time which to many appear incurable.

Egon Heckeroth writes:

God speaks though His intermediaries, when men have reached
a crisis and see no apparent way out. We have only to think of the
now widespread efforts to repair the world through partial

reforms and thus reduce the problems. Despite increasing efforts on all levels of social life, no one has succeeded in bringing calm and composure to mankind. Partial reforms do *not* lead to the renewal of the whole! Only he who is whole in himself can also renew the whole from the ground up. But who is whole in himself? This wholeness can be ascribed to God alone.

He *alone* is capable of renewing His Creation, from the ground up, from its very basis and source, and thence into a new phase of development.[11]

The followers of Bahá'u'lláh are filled with confidence that the time is ripe for the realisation of universal peace. Here Bahá'ís are distinct from many who, though they desire peace, can see no possibility of its realisation within the foreseeable future. Through belief in Bahá'u'lláh and his creative word Bahá'ís develop into a human type filled with longing for and firm faith in peace. 'Peace on earth' to them is the content of faith and the goal of all action and this in itself is the first step to success.

This first essential step consists in many people attaching themselves to the transmuting, hope-dispensing river of faith in the feasibility of peace, not allowing themselves to be misled hither and thither by dreary everyday life and warmongering, or to be persuaded that everything must stay as it is. We must liberate ourselves from our wretched entanglement with all kinds of prejudice, racism, nationalism and religious restrictiveness, and come ultimately to the knowledge of the world-embracing, the essential and the unified. Without *religious renewal* this is ultimately impossible.

I would like to clarify this by means of examples: in the late 60s the Catholic Cardinal Spellman and the Protestant Pastor Niemöller had completely opposing views on the Vietnam War. Today the Catholic Church in the USA and in the Federal Republic of Germany have adopted opposing views on the NATO dual track decision. Even from reading Alt's book and the various replies it has aroused, it becomes clear that in Christianity, just as in the rest of the world, there are *no binding, undisputed criteria* for the shaping of the future.

If we compare Bahá'ís with this, we find that the substance of their faith and their lives is to create the unity of mankind within the framework of Bahá'u'lláh's world order. Not for one moment do they doubt that this goal will be achieved. What distinguishes Bahá'ís is that they are united in their outlook on all the fundamental questions of this world. All the essential standards and norms for the harmonious, peaceful coexistence of an organically united mankind are unmistakably clear, even in some cases to the practical details revealed in the Holy Scriptures of the Bahá'í Faith; a Bahá'í can neither ignore them nor minimise their significance. For the individual Bahá'í they represent the fundamentals of his faith. Everyone who believes in Bahá'u'lláh accepts these doctrines and principles without any ifs and buts. If, however, the person concerned were to join a group of Christians he would have to expect his good impulses and work for the peace and harmony of mankind to be neutralised by other Christian groups who from their own standpoint are motivated by the noblest arguments.

It is a fatal fallacy to believe that a civilisation for mankind might be built up on a plurality of fundamental values.

4. *All people must independently seek the truth* – including and especially religious truth. They should not blindly take over traditional or new faiths. A world civilisation calls for citizens who free themselves from the habits and precon-

ceptions which inhibit intellectual and spiritual progress and impede world unity, and who seek the truth with determination and a critical mind.

This demand is essential, because preconceptions hamper the irrefutable growth of contact between peoples, races and religions and are a hindrance to the goal of unification. *We can and must all learn from each other.* We can also learn from primitive peoples, and experience a new dimension of enrichment. The minorities, which have unfortunately always been suppressed in the story of mankind so far, must be not only tolerated but positively encouraged. Since we are not of ourselves always in a position to recognise our weaknesses and prejudices, let alone to overcome them, we must adapt our thinking and feeling to the new yardsticks established for us by the Divine Revealer in our age, Bahá'u'lláh. Despite our earnest endeavours, it will take a few generations to achieve the universal openness necessary to success.

5. *Religion must be the cause of unity and harmony among people*, never a reason for schism. If a religion leads to conflict or injustice, its essence must have been afflicted and it is no longer in keeping with the times.

The Universal House of Justice comments:

Indeed, one of the strangest and saddest features of the current outbreak of religious fanaticism is the extent to which, in each case, it is undermining not only the spiritual values which are conducive to the unity of mankind but also those unique moral victories won by the particular religion it purports to serve.[12]

6. *Religion must be in harmony with science and reason.*
Religion and science must complement each other and must not ultimately be contradictory. They are the two aspects of the one indivisible truth. Man is like a bird, using

the two wings of faith and reason. He flies best (makes progress in the material and spiritual spheres) when both wings are strong and in balance. Value-free science without religious and moral attachment fosters materialism and may lead to universal catastrophe. On the other hand, a faith that is hostile to reason leads to superstition and fanaticism, which in turn results in the disunity and self-torture of humanity. Both individual and social development are at their best when the two wings of truth – faith and reason – complement one another.

In Chapter 3 I described how in the new age we shall participate in the integral consciousness, beyond mental consciousness. Accordingly the dualisms strongly influenced by our mental consciousness will be dispersed and even overcome. I explained on pages 22 and 36 that in the Bahá'í religion there is no absolute evil. Evil is the absence of good, just as darkness is the absence of light. This view is wholly biblical: we have only to think of the very concrete exhortation 'Overcome evil with good'. [13] Within the integral consciousness, religion and science are seen not as opposites but as supplementary to a greater unity. For this reason it is interesting that 'Abdu'l-Bahá defines both religion and nature as the absolutely 'necessary relations derived from the realities of things', while love is 'the vital bond' inherent in them. [14] Here too we see a fundamental reconciliation where there was once a major seed of strife!

7. *Men and women have equal rights*. Practically this means that the question of equality of education and opportunity for the female sex takes precedence worldwide. The Universal House of Justice describes the achievement of full equality between the sexes as 'one of the most important, though less acknowledged prerequisites of peace'.

The denial of such equality perpetrates an injustice against one half of the world's population and promotes in men harmful attitudes and habits that are carried from the family to the workplace, to political life, and ultimately to international relations. There are no grounds, moral, practical, or biological, upon which such denial can be justified. Only as women are welcomed into full partnership in all fields of human endeavour will the moral and psychological climate be created in which international peace can emerge.[15]

Better education and training of women are directly beneficial to the next generation, since after all the mothers are the first educators of their children. If in particular cases the means for the education and training of the children of both sexes are inadequate, the girls should be given preference. The equal status of women is the touchstone for a mature, unprejudiced society which has given up discriminating against or suppressing any group on the basis of biological differences. Some may object that principles such as the equality of the sexes are axiomatic and there is no reason for a new religion to have to proclaim such principles. However:

a. This principle – like the other principles of the Bahá'í Faith – was established 120 years ago, at a time when it was not axiomatic anywhere in the world.

b. Even today most of the world has failed to enshrine the equality of the sexes either in law or in social practice.

c. No religion other than the Bahá'í acknowledges this principle, because earlier ages were not ready for it. It is interesting to observe that even in Christian countries this principle of the equality of the sexes has increasingly come into legal and social practice as these countries have been exposed to secularisation and humanist tendencies. Equality accordingly diminishes in Europe from Sweden to Spain. I certainly do not need to cite examples from the Islamic countries. So it is particularly important from a religious standpoint to know that a new founder of religion has created reliable guidelines here for everyone.

8. *Education and training* are vital.
The best possible education for both sexes was commended by Bahá'u'lláh to parents and society as their supreme task and duty: the intellectual, spiritual and physical evolution of the human being, the capacity to promote a constantly advancing culture and civilisation.

The cause of universal education, which has already enlisted in its service an army of dedicated people from every faith and nation, deserves the utmost support that the governments of the world can lend it. For ignorance is indisputably the principal reason for the decline and fall of peoples and the perpetuation of prejudice . . . In keeping with the requirements of the times, consideration should also be given to teaching the concept of world citizenship as part of the standard education of every child.[16]

Special regard is paid in the Bahá'í Faith to the profession of the teacher and educator. Bahá'u'lláh's key to the division of inheritance gives teachers a share in the deceased's estate – a bold, revolutionary recommendation which on closer inspection is seen to be quite consistent. In the age of the maturity of mankind not only blood relatives are remembered, but also the communicators of the things of the mind.

9. *Social problems must be resolved on the basis of universal justice.* All the resources of the world must be exploited for the benefit of mankind as a whole. Poverty must be removed; poor, disadvantaged nations must be given a

standard of living commensurate with human dignity through a kind of worldwide system of compensation. Efficient performance must be given well-balanced encouragement in every continent. The many sick people whose diseases are caused by poverty and ignorance must also be healed through the common efforts of humanity. This development must not be compelled by force but must be brought about by appropriate social education and legislation, without giving rise to further injustices. We are used to paying taxes for our own community, our county and our state; why not for our world?

The Universal House of Justice has taken stock of the situation in these terms:

The time has come when those who preach the dogmas of materialism, whether of the east or the west, whether of capitalism or socialism, must give account of the moral stewardship they have presumed to exercise. Where is the 'new world' promised by these ideologies? Where is the international peace to whose ideals they proclaim their devotion? Where are the breakthroughs into new realms of cultural achievement produced by the aggrandizement of this race, of that nation or of a particular class? Why is the vast majority of the world's people sinking ever deeper into hunger and wretchedness when wealth on a scale undreamed of by the Pharaohs, the Caesars, or even the imperialist powers of the nineteenth century is at the disposal of the present arbiters of human affairs?[17]

From the Bahá'í viewpoint, the reason why capitalism and communism have equally suffered shipwreck is that both philosophical systems lack spiritual components. In the Western world there is too much enthusiasm for liberalism, with the belief that the economy is best served by leaving everything to market forces. Insufficient consideration is given to the fact that a functioning market calls for equal ranking partners who keep to basic rules; otherwise it can easily develop into a slave market. How else can one explain the fact that in recent years in the United States at a time of economic boom, the numbers of the poor, that is those who live below the bread-line, has risen from 9 to 11 per cent of the whole population?

An industrious nation of 17 millions, like Nepal, exports annually to the value of some 20 million pounds in order to obtain the necessary foreign currency for the purchase of capital goods abroad – just about the sum a famous pop singer paid his third wife in alimony.

On my last visit to China I met a German who was making a lot of money by selling human hair, of regular thickness and colour and measuring twenty centimetres, for 5 dollars per kilo. How fortunate that there is no demand for human skin; that too would otherwise undoubtedly be offered at slave-market prices.

The elimination of poverty and the restriction of wealth within the framework of the unity of the world is the Bahá'í Faith's option for the economy.

10. All schools will teach *in addition to the mother tongue a world auxiliary language* and a standard script as a basis for direct understanding between all the inhabitants of the world.

The introduction of a world auxiliary language is of immense importance to the spiritual and cultural evolution of mankind. Overcoming the language barriers by introducing a universal language is an essential building block in the coming world civilisation. At the same time, existing languages must be nurtured and promoted. Symbolically the world auxiliary language means an end to the Babylonian confusion of tongues in the Kingdom of Peace.

'Unity and peace are the attainable goal towards which humanity is striving', concludes the Universal House of Justice.

The experience of the Bahá'í community may be seen as an example of this enlarging unity. It is a community of some three to four million people drawn from many nations, cultures, classes and creeds, engaged in a wide range of activities serving the spiritual, social and economic needs of the peoples of many lands. It is a single social organism, representative of the diversity of the human family, conducting its affairs through a system of commonly accepted consultative principles and cherishing equally all the great outpourings of divine guidance in human history. Its existence is yet another convincing proof of the practicality of its Founder's vision of a united world, another evidence that humanity can live as one global society, equal to whatever challenges its coming of age may entail. If the Bahá'í experience can contribute in whatever measure to reinforcing hope in the unity of the human race, we are happy to offer it as a model for study.[18]

SIX

Thy Kingdom Come

We convey to you not only a vision in words: we summon the power of deeds of faith and sacrifice.[1]

Since the Islamic Government was established in Iran in 1979 there is no end to the reports of the persecution and suppression of Bahá'ís. Many have lost their rights as citizens. They are imprisoned without cause, lose their work or their pensions, are prevented from attending schools or universities, see their businesses and houses plundered, burned or expropriated and their cemeteries levelled. Bahá'í marriages are annulled and their children declared illegitimate. With or without the process of law Bahá'ís are shot, hanged, burned alive or otherwise tortured to death. The targets of the greatest persecution are the members of the Spiritual Assemblies. A Spiritual Assembly, whether national or local, consists of nine elected members. The members of the National Spiritual Assembly of the Bahá'ís in Iran were kidnapped and to this day nothing is known of their fate. When a new Assembly was subsequently formed, its members were also imprisoned and shot after torture. Similarly, in

Teheran and the main cities of Iran, in Tabriz, Shiraz, Hamadan and Yazd, the members of the local Assemblies have been liquidated, often after cruel torture.

The atrocities past and present, practised in part secretly but in part quite officially, against this, Iran's largest religious minority, have led to declarations of solidarity and sympathy throughout the world. Leading figures such as King Baudouin of Belgium, President Reagan, Indira Gandhi, President Mitterrand, the German Federal Foreign Minister Hans-Dietrich Genscher and many other public figures have appealed publicly to the Iranian Government to undertake to put an end to the repression of the Bahá'ís in Iran. The General Assembly of the United Nations, the UN Human Rights Commission, the Council of Europe, the European Parliament, many centres of government and parliaments of different countries, as well as Amnesty International, have espoused the cause of the Bahá'ís in Iran and strongly condemned their persecution.[2]

The Islamic Government in Iran has now banned the activities of the Spiritual Assemblies. From loyalty to the government – an important principle of the Bahá'í Faith – the Persian Bahá'ís have yielded to this injustice and dissolved a total of 500 local Spiritual Assemblies as well as the National Spiritual Assembly of the Bahá'ís in Iran.

The Rule of the Meek

What is a *Spiritual Assembly*, this target of the Islamic priesthood? To Bahá'ís the Spiritual Assembly is the missing link between the commandments of the Sermon on the Mount for the individual and the structures, committed to justice, of a world order for the whole of mankind. It is therefore claimed that through the selection and operation of these institutions, in the course of development morality will successfully be integrated with politics.[3]

Previous history has been characterised by the rule of those who feel called upon to impress their will on the community. The appalling arbitrariness of individual tyrants is no doubt largely a thing of the past. Nevertheless, even the present democracies and people's democracies are influenced by the struggle between strong personalities and interest groups; power and its exercise predominate. The individual stands, or in other words he is nominated by the party or an interest group, to praise his own qualities in an election and to prevail against other candidates, with whom he tends to deal far from delicately. If elected, he is more or less committed to the party or interest group which has helped him to power. Parties and interests are nowadays the framework within which a politician develops. This type of selection is an expression of our political culture. For the struggle against others, however stylised it may be, belligerent characters with few scruples are needed.

Partiality and the representation of interests must give way to the goal of a just world order, in which a worthy human existence is to be made available to everyone, regardless of race or creed. The goal of world order is God-given. From its inception it produces radical changes: people will not stoop to make their point by force and will have as little taste for the present fashion of political struggle as we have today for the gladiatorial battles of the late Roman era. And so, step by step, the promised rule of the meek will be established.

We need new political structures. Just as the transition from absolutism to the present-day democracies and people's democracies was a process of development of political culture, so too the new political structures which pacify the world as a whole must be provided with enormous depth and must correspond in our current awareness with ethical standards and the perfection of human dignity.

Proceeding from the insight that mankind is now advancing towards the stage of maturity, Bahá'ís offer universal literacy, politically speaking, instead of the incapacitating single party of Communism and instead of the multi-party system of the Western democracies, directed towards false, limited goals. The individual is involved far more intensively than before in shaping the political will.

If you like, every individual is a party. The real parliament is established in the regular meeting of local Bahá'í communities (Nineteen Day Feast). Every Bahá'í, young or old, man or woman, scholar or illiterate, is summoned nineteen times a year to participate and has the opportunity to contribute proposals and advice on all matters concerning the community, the country and the world. The Bahá'í is prepared for this task of contributing to the welfare of society by studying the creative Word of God, which has to be related, as a yardstick and source of motivation, to all the events of life, both personal and social. This communal meeting envisaged by Bahá'u'lláh differs from Sunday Church attendance in the following ways, in particular:

a. Worship is organised by the Spiritual Assembly. Since

there is no priestly class in the Bahá'í Faith, no single personality is central and there is no sermon in the old sense.

b. After worship information is exchanged, the Spiritual Assembly informing the community of its decisions, especially in connection with the proposals studied at previous general meetings. This is followed by a general discussion of points brought forward by those present, often with recommendations and proposals to the Spiritual Assembly.

c. The third part of the Nineteen Day Feast is devoted to the strengthening of social bonds through informal conversation and refreshments.

At its regular meetings for the Nineteen Day Feast, the community not only finds a source of edification and discussion but also forms a group in which experience shows that more attention is paid to altruistic moral activity than in the anonymity of industrial urban society. This development enables it to avoid the major disadvantage of modern civilisation, the outstanding feature of which is that people have become socially isolated from each other. In his administrative and social order Bahá'u'lláh undertook to create social bonds in which the willingness voluntarily to observe common standards is incomparably greater. These Nineteen Day Feasts are not the result of theoretical appraisals; they are an institution of Bahá'u'lláh practised by Bahá'ís in every country in the world. In Teheran, where before the Islamic Government ban there were over 60,000 Bahá'ís, more than 200 Nineteen Day Feasts took place simultaneously.

Elections – But How?

It is not the individual who cries: 'I am the best and the most suitable', nor does any party or interest group nominate the man who best serves that party or interest group; rather it is God who, for the realisation of His will, uses the community to elect people whose aim is the *good of the whole*, who enjoy people's confidence and are capable of developing the necessary spiritual and practical abilities. This administrative and social order evolved by Bahá'ís is, according to its structure, to serve as a model for adoption by the world. In every village and in every town where nine or more Bahá'ís live, they annually elect their *Spiritual Assembly*, consisting of nine people who take on the leadership and administration of the community for a year. To promote candidates or to extol suitable people from one's own standpoint is forbidden.

Bahá'í elections differ from the usual election in various ways: The elections have a strong religious and spiritual component. They are secret, in accordance with the idea that in the silence of prayer God may assist the elector to make the right decision. For Bahá'ís it is axiomatic that even marriage partners should not discuss which names they will write on the election slip. During the year each Bahá'í takes note of figures in the community who live their life according to their religion, developing spiritual and practical capacities, and who are thoroughly experienced. Active or passive candidature is not permitted, let alone vociferous election campaigning.

It might be objected that this model is not transferable to nations but works best in a small context. Here are some comments:

a. The Bahá'í concept of elections differs qualitatively from modern democratic concepts. This is not simply a question of method. In the context of the present-day structures in the world, Bahá'í elections have no chance as yet of taking place among the masses.

b. But if we do not put new wine in old bottles, if we believe in the educability of human beings by the Revealer and see this belief as the new Ark for the salvation of mankind, then we find that this enhancement of the quality of the election system is realistic, because for the elector the observance of ethical standards in politics is steadily gaining ground. Can one see in the traditional democratic election battles an attempt to found the Kingdom of God on earth?

The councils thus elected at local, national and international level, though responsible only to their own conscience, are, however, linked in constant exchange and communication with the base.

The model is already operating, both in the bush and in the university town. Even if a degree of education on the lines of the new model, as well as the observation of fundamental spiritual and ethical principles, considerably increases the efficiency of the new structures, nevertheless the application of sections of the Bahá'í model is capable even now of enriching many social spheres: works committee elections, parent meetings, the elections and discussions in church communities, town halls, etc. At all events, this offer should not be lightly dismissed. One per thousand of mankind – that is the size of the Bahá'í world community today, with a strongly upward trend – are gathering experience of this new model.

Bahá'í Consultation

One of the cornerstones in the construction of the Kingdom of God on earth is a consultation worthy of the name. It is a main pillar of Bahá'u'lláh's World Order and at the same time an essential constituent of religious life. In the community gathering that takes place worldwide every nineteen days among Bahá'ís – every Bahá'í is bound to take part – the consultative element is central. *Every Bahá'í* in the world thus has a platform from which to submit proposals which have or might achieve local, national or international significance, and to contribute to their discussion.

This worldwide Bahá'í practice of constant involvement of *everyone* in the consultation process is a step towards universal literacy and a key element in the coming world civilisation. The technique of Bahá'í consultation[4] has been for decades in accordance with the most up-to-date research findings:

1. Ascertaining the facts and agreeing on them.
2. Agreement on the spiritual or administrative principles associated with the problem.
3. Comprehensive, open discussion of the matter, leading to a proposed solution.
4. Agreement on the decision.

However, a real improvement in the quality of consultation is dependent on a relevant spiritual and religious education. Some characteristics:

– The spiritual attitude in consultation and in prayer is similar. One must not be dazzled by personal opinions and suggestions but must always remain receptive. The contribution to the discussion is presented with extreme openness and courtesy and with no attempt to press one's case, manipulate or mobilise those of like mind. My personal experience after years of serving as a member of Bahá'í Spiritual Assemblies gives me confidence that the *art of spiritually motivated consultation* is learnable insofar as the relevant education is available and the general framework for it is at hand. As long as the spiritual atmosphere of the discussion can be maintained (even in material and difficult matters such as budgets or divorce), the results achieved are excellent and strengthen the common bond between those concerned.

– The members of the decision-making body must always be aware of their dependence on God and ask that God's will should take shape through them, even in lesser matters. That is why spiritual recollection and worship precede every Bahá'í consultation. Both in the discussion and in the elections we must reject the corrupt, egotistical, divisive practices of our materialist age and place spiritual values at the centre of our thought and action. Shoghi Effendi writes:

Nothing short of the spirit of earnest and sustained consultation . . . nothing less than persistent and strenuous warfare against our own instincts and natural inclinations, and heroic self-sacrifice in subordinating our own likings to the imperative requirements of the Cause of God, can insure our undivided loyalty to so sacred a principle – a principle that will for all time safeguard our beloved Cause from the allurements and the trivialities of the world without, and of the pitfalls of the self within.[5]

Bahá'í Worship

Another stone in the mosaic of the Bahá'í model is

worship. As we said, the priestly class was abolished by
Bahá'u'lláh because we are entering into the age of
maturity of mankind. The independent search for truth
contains a universal dimension for everyone, and every
individual Bahá'í has the spiritual obligation to pray
daily. In the Houses of Worship of the Bahá'ís in every
continent[6] there are readings from the Holy Scriptures of
all the great religions, without commentary or exegesis.
Differing viewpoints and insights, as well as explana-
tions, are dealt with outside the House of Worship, in
lectures, seminars and discussions. The House of
Worship is reserved for the word of God alone, whether
spoken or sung, as a symbol of the disarming of
theology, which in the past distorted the Cause of God to
its own ends and destroyed the unity of the community
by denominationalism and sectarianism.

As envisaged by Bahá'u'lláh, the House of Worship
stands for the fundamental unity of religions and of the
Divine Manifestations who were their spokesmen. At
the same time it is the spiritual focus for each
community, surrounded by social, charitable, cultural
and scholarly institutions. Schools, old people's homes,
hospitals, etc, should be sited close to the House of
Worship. It is interesting to know that the financing of all
Bahá'í projects depends on voluntary contributions to
the various funds by Bahá'ís only.[7]

The Dissemination of the Faith

The Bahá'í Faith today comprises barely one per
thousand of the human population. There are about a
dozen countries in which the proportion of Bahá'ís to the
population as a whole exceeds one per cent. The area now

occupying the top position, with 15% of Bahá'ís to the whole population, is Tuvalu in the Pacific, almost the furthest point from Iran, its land of origin.

In Iran itself, 2% of the population of Islamic origin have adopted the Bahá'í Faith, but many more of the religious minorities: of the Persian Zoroastrians and Jews, some 20% have become Bahá'ís. And yet these minorities have a particularly difficult time. Not only Bahá'u'lláh but also Muhammad and Christ, Buddha and Krishna must be taken into their hearts and minds and accepted unconditionally. Apparently it is easier for those who both geographically and in their religious history have the longer roads to travel, to find their way to the Bahá'í Faith.

Conversion is voluntary, never by force. The principle that all people should be free to seek truth independently, especially religious truth, applies particularly to Bahá'ís in their efforts to disseminate their beliefs (see above, p. 76). Moreover, Bahá'ís are enjoined under Bahá'í law to respect and protect the rights of minorities where they themselves form the majority.

There are Bahá'ís living in more than 110,000 places in the world. There are more than 30,000 Spiritual Assemblies. Worldwide, 143 National Spiritual Assemblies are at work. Bahá'í literature has been translated into 739 languages and dialects. Believers from 2,100 different minority groups and tribes have now come under the banner of Bahá'u'lláh.

Bahá'u'lláh created a network of connections which contribute to the integration of the members of various different races, nationalities and cultures within a common world system. Above and beyond the teachings associated with a unified mankind, the laws and commandments of Bahá'u'lláh, such as praying and fasting, use of a common calendar, the celebration of common feast-days and others, help to create a world conscience which is neither oriental nor occidental. The Bahá'í Faith can be counted today as 'one of the fastest-growing' religious communities.[8]

The Bahá'ís and the Future

These details are evidence that Bahá'ís all over the world are taking educational and practical steps to fulfil the great task of uniting humanity in accordance with spiritual and moral standards. *The ways of change are manifest in things that seem quite small.* Certainly many other groups, cults and sects enjoy more widespread popularity than the Bahá'í Faith, but there are a number of facts which, even from a scientific standpoint, give me the confidence and certainty that the Bahá'í Faith will prevail in the long-term future:

1. The Bahá'í movement is indisputably an independent religion, which means that it is a phenomenon unique in the history of religion since the foundation of Islam approximately 1360 years ago.[9]

2. A universal responsiveness distinguishes the Bahá'í Faith from sects and groupings which separate from a main church and claim to be the true representatives of the mother religion. The circle of supporters of such sects is essentially restricted to converts from the mother religion, whereas for the faith of Bahá'u'lláh such restrictions do not exist. To put it another way, while the Adventists and Jehovah's Witnesses are virtually unable to win supporters among Muslims or Buddhists, it is difficult to say whether in the Bahá'í world there are now

more Bahá'ís with a Hindu, Christian or Islamic
background. Like every original revealed religion, the
Bahá'í Faith has the capacity to address the human being,
regardless of the civilisation he inhabits, his social class,
education and religious affiliation. To historians and
sociologists such as Arnold Toynbee and Jacques
Chouleur,[10] this universalism is sufficient reason to
recognise the Bahá'í Faith as the possible world religion
of the future.

3. While the various religious movements of the modern
age are concerned with the 'old truths', trying to find
their way back to pure Christianity, Islam or Hinduism,
the Bahá'í Faith is essentially future-orientated. As the
plenipotentiary divine legislator, Bahá'u'lláh fulfils the
promise: 'Behold, I make all things new.'[11] Bahá'ís are
privileged to collaborate in shaping this new creation, the
greatest spiritual adventure in human history.

SEVEN

Thy Will Be Done on Earth

Bend your minds and wills to the education of the peoples and kindreds of the earth, that haply the dissensions that divide it may, through the power of the Most Great Name, be blotted out from its face, and all mankind become the upholders of one Order, and the inhabitants of one City.[1]

Man's confrontation with the second death, that is the possibility of the collective death of mankind, gives a new dimension not only to war but also to peace. Previous peace treaties have been short-lived, lasting in rare cases for decades or a generation. Today mankind must create enduring peace; starting with the Lesser Peace the peoples, nations, races and religions must move towards the Most Great Peace. This means that at the same time a worldwide process of pacification of the people must be initiated, which will gradually lead to the healing of the sick body of mankind. Universal love must constantly gain in intensity in the context of a just world order, enabling people to develop increasingly a world conscience which makes war unthinkable. Through this, conflicts can be settled and resolved before they endanger the life of humanity.

This universal peace must embrace all areas of the political, economic, social and religious life of mankind and must fulfil the fundamental doctrine of the unity of mankind.

In order to have our share of peace we have to give up some holy cows. In the political area, parts of our national sovereignty must be transferred to a federal world state. The United Nations Organisation can be regarded as the germ cell of this future state. It is a great mistake to believe that in the international contest every one of the 150 nations of the world can win the position corresponding to its capacities and status through its own initiative. The market does not operate here; markets can operate when the external conditions are in harmony, for instance when the contestants have similar starting conditions.

It is impossible to pacify the world as long as the nations can act in accordance with selfish national interests. Since the Second World War scarcely a single country in the Third World has succeeded in permanently improving its status, although experiments have been made with various forms of government and there have even been bloody revolutions as well. On the whole, the gap between rich and poor countries has in fact grown from decade to decade. Even the willingness of rich countries to contribute to development aid is fading in the face of these unhealthy developments.

Many people feel instinctively that existing methods do not lead to world peace because they are not based on a *single, unified* world. It may still seem understandable that this elementary fact is not taken into account by politicians, each caught in his own selfishly national net. But it is dismaying that even those who are guided by ethical standards and seeking spiritual and religious solutions fail to see the obvious. Why do not the various peace movements write *World Unity*, in the sense of a federal world state, on their banners? No doubt because the prospect is too big, too fantastic – so fantastic, so big, that only a new world religion with its own form of consciousness is capable of handling it at all.

Many people believe that only the politicians have the capacity to create peace. If only the politicians were a little more human, a little more reasonable, they would sit down at a table and conclude treaties which would ensure the peace and quiet of mankind. In my opinion, this is quite erroneous. The whole of mankind must co-operate in building world peace. Consciously or unconsciously, every one of us is an amalgam of inherited or acquired prejudices: religious, national, racial prejudices, etc.

Even the basic pattern of our thinking, even the human images which predominate today in the various religions, are very far from geared to the coming peaceful world. Day after day priests and princes of the church throughout the hierarchy appeal to the politicians to make peace – certainly a matter of necessity, indeed of life and death. One can only hope that the politicians addressed are not church-goers, for in the churches they will often learn that man has been broken off at the root and is incapable of escaping the compulsion to sin. In this context, peace itself is not expected in this life, only in the hereafter.

When one thinks of the centuries throughout which

this image of man has been transmitted to the faithful, it is no wonder that in the Christian West there are strong spiritual reservations against peace. The scale of scepticism and pessimism is beyond description, so great that many thinking people reject the idea of the unity of mankind lock, stock and barrel, while others perceive universal reconciliation as a potential loss of identity.

It is often forgotten that identity itself is progressive. Few English people know today whether they are descended from the Vikings, the Picts, the Celts, the Saxons or the Normans. Nor are other Europeans any more able to reconstruct their tribal membership. Is this connected with a loss of identity? One is filled with bitterness when one observes that over the centuries the blood of millions has flowed in the name of this alleged identity.

What is generally feared as a loss of identity is in reality an expanded self-awareness, a new identity. Each Divine Revealer brings to mankind an enhanced sense of identity. It is the lack of consciousness of the new identity that cuts us off from our future. Now we have to find our way to this new identity, to see and organise this planet as the native country of us all. Our true identity is not as 'Vandals', 'cannibals' or 'hunters and gatherers' but as 'members of a world civilisation'. Nor must we regard people who live on the far side of a river or a mountain as foreigners, opponents or enemies. This is an essential condition for the creation of peace, since it must engage not only our reason but also our hearts and minds.

Our true identity is spiritually, not geographically based. We must not divide men as the wool merchant divides sheep: merinos from the Australian plains here, Karakul mountain sheep from the Caucasus there. We must light our lamps from the lamp of the Prince of Peace, then we shall no longer be able to regard any inhabitant of Earth as a foreigner. Our true identity does not lie in the past but in the future. We are not moving from the roots *via* the branches to the leaves, we are on our way from the periphery towards the centre.

In the material sphere the father comes first, then the son. In the spiritual and religious sphere, on the other hand, the Son came first and the Father is coming today. It is our privilege to be living in the Day of God, and that is our time, as described in the Holy Scriptures of all the major religions. It is our privilege to discover our planetary, universal identity and to erect upon it the mansion of the unity of mankind. Political peace is only one aspect of this unity. 'Abdu'l-Bahá, son of the founder of the Bahá'í Faith, lists seven 'candles of unity', seven areas which together make up unity:[2]

1. Unity in the political realm.
2. Unity of thought in world undertakings.
3. Unity in freedom.
4. Unity in religion.
5. Unity of nations.
6. Unity of races.
7. Unity of language.

In the religious field the holy cow that has to be given up is religious demarcation. Theologians of the different religions have left no stone unturned, no avenue unexplored, in teaching their followers, from the cradle onwards, to see their *own* faith as the most pleasing to God and their *own* Divine Messengers as the highest-ranking. Even *within* the denominations and sects, every believer is convinced that *his* way and *his* belief is the best. The fact that today God has offered universal reconcili-

ation through Bahá'u'lláh, in which we can without
reservation recognise other people as 'brothers in truth',
produces rejection instead of joyful relief among theologians of all religions and provenances. But what we need
today is *universal* love, which is more than love of
neighbour and one's enemy.

Bahá'u'lláh has already transmitted to a small part of
the *whole* of mankind, in terms of this universal love, a
new vision that makes life worth living. Sociologically it
is interesting that in all essential universal matters,
through Bahá'u'lláh, a broad cross-section of humanity
from the most varied racial, national and religious
backgrounds is unfolding a new conscience, sharing the
same ideals and standards. From the viewpoint of many
religious scholars the Bahá'í Faith has stood the test. The
sociologist Christine Hakim, who is a Bahá'í, writes on
its practical results:

Certain development trends in the international Bahá'í
community can be clearly defined; for instance, advances in
the education of women on their way to equal rights, and a
higher degree of literacy in the Bahá'í communities; in
particular, the integration of different classes of the population
within the solid unity of the Bahá'í communities contributes
to overcoming problems such as the caste problem in India,
racial prejudices in the United States and other countries, the
generation gulf in Europe, the tribal feuds in Africa. The larger
these religious communities are, the more visible the social
progress of the whole becomes.[3]

Ninety years after Bahá'u'lláh's passing, there is no
more debate among the religious scholars as to whether
the Bahá'í Faith is an original religion of revelation. I
know that for Christians special importance attaches to

Jesus's words: 'I am the way, the truth and the life; no man cometh to the Father but by me.'[4] But these words could be used to reject every religious claim at any time, without further examination. To comment briefly on this theme: absoluteness, uniqueness and matchlessness exclude repetition, but in abundant statements and parables Jesus spoke to His disciples and prepared them for *His return*.

a. Most Christians therefore await the Second Coming of the Lord. How and in what form this Coming will take place is of course disputed by theologians. The question is: on His return, may Christ assert of Himself: 'I am the way, the truth and the life' – or may He not?

b. If Bahá'u'lláh's doctrine of the unity of the founders of religions is correct, then logically each of them must correctly describe himself as the Truth, as alpha and omega. It is the same sun, rising from a different point. It is interesting to observe that all founders of religions have claimed the same or similar attributes for themselves as Christ.[5]

c. Does the Peace Movement really believe that a tolerant, humanist superstructure can be strong enough to maintain peaceful co-existence for ever among followers of different religions, each claiming the absolute, unique and matchless nature of its own founder and hence of their own religions?

In *Nathan the Wise* the German philosopher Lessing immortalised the idea of tolerance in the famous parable of the ring. A king gives a ring to his sons, charging them to keep it safely, for whoever owns it will be his successor. When the time comes, each of the sons produces a ring. Which is genuine? When the judge has examined the rings and heard the statements of each son, he exhorts them to mutual tolerance, but he leaves the last judgement to a 'true Judge' who will come 'in a thousand years'. Lessing felt that the last word had not yet been spoken on the relationship between the religions.

Bahá'u'lláh's judgement is that all 'rings' are undoubtedly absolutely genuine. Each of the sons must acknowledge the authenticity of the others' rings as well as his own. Religious tolerance will thus be superseded and crowned by the unity of religions.

The classification of other religions from the viewpoint of one's own religion can be divided into four basic types:

The first type is orthodox rejection, as was customary only a few decades ago in Christianity and is still the case today in many religious communities. Other religions are said to be of the devil and their founders false prophets.

The second type is tolerant acceptance, to be met with in various Christian churches today. The other religions may contain traces of the revealed truth, their founders may be outstanding and deeply religious personalities, but the fullness of the unique truth is to be found only in one's own religion. However, the other standpoint is tolerated with resignation or perhaps sometimes with a bad grace.

The third type, as represented by the well-known Catholic theologian Hans Küng, is tolerance with recognition:

– that we Christians can no longer regard Islam as a way to hell, as it was in previous Catholic doctrine and is even now for many conservative Protestant churches – but as one possible way to eternal life, an interpretation which has been possible for Catholics since Vatican II but is still controversial in the World Council of Churches. So Islam too is one of the ways of salvation.

– that we must no longer regard the prophet Muhammad as a false prophet but must accept, as serious theologians, his productive prophetic function for monotheistic belief among hundreds of millions of people living in the vast spaces of North Africa and from Soviet Uzbekistan to Indonesia: so Muhammad is a post-Christian prophet, a 'Warner' of the one God of Abraham;

– that we must by no means discredit the Qur'án nowadays as a deviant mixture of old Arabian-Judaeo-Christian ideas but should put its factually obvious power as the Word of God for the faithful into its proper light, with understanding: the Qur'án is the effective Word of the all-merciful, compassionate God for Muslim believers.[6]

The nuances should be noted. Islam – Qur'án – Muhammad represent the truth, for Muslim believers at least. Küng's tolerance has exposed him to the accusation of having abandoned his Christian foundations.

The fourth type is the Bahá'í standpoint of the fundamental unity of the religions and their founders. There is *one* religion of God, whose representatives differ only in place and time in terms of a progressive divine revelation. The outpouring of revelation corresponds to the cultural and spiritual development of each era.

This is an unreserved Yes to all religions. Those who do not fully acknowledge other religions are warned by Bahá'u'lláh in these terms:

Beware, O believers in the Unity of God, lest ye be tempted to make any distinction between any of the Manifestations of His

Cause, or to discriminate against the signs that have accompanied and proclaimed their Revelation. This indeed is the true meaning of Divine Unity, if ye be of them that apprehend and believe this truth. Be ye assured, moreover, that the works and acts of each and every one of these Manifestations of God, nay whatever pertaineth unto them, and whatsoever they may manifest in the future, are all ordained by God and are a reflection of His Will and Purpose. Whoso maketh the slightest possible difference between their persons, their words, their messages, their acts and manners, hath indeed disbelieved in God, hath repudiated His signs and betrayed the Cause of His Messengers.[7]

As all religions teach, man is made in the image of God. In accordance with this terminology, what else can the *Kingdom of God on earth* mean but a structure of order among human beings, sustained by divine principles, a world order, which fulfils spiritual and religious, ethical and moral standards? Since the unification of mankind has both organisational and strong emotional components, this unification may be better effected by a religion which is still free of historical encumbrances. In the history of the Bahá'í Faith, in which there has been no lack of violent turbulence,[8] fire and the sword play no role. In no case has any attempt been made to disseminate the faith by non-peaceful means. Bahá'ís have always observed Bahá'u'lláh's commandment to be killed rather than to kill. Despite crying injustices suffered by the Bahá'í community in Iran in the last 140 years, and still suffered today, scarcely any cases are known in which Bahá'ís have killed others for the sake of the faith, or have become terrorists. Even when accusations of all kinds have been made against Bahá'ís in state-managed campaigns (alleging espionage on behalf of one foreign power or another), no evidence of guilt could ever be produced.

People in Europe find it extraordinarily difficult to believe that the banner of lasting peace can be raised only by a new religious Founder. But we may ask: do not the followers of all religions await a Prince of Peace who will appear in the fullness of time and through whose works swords will be turned into ploughshares? And here I ask: Is not the time fulfilled?

We must agree unreservedly with Carl-Friedrich von Weizsäcker when he writes:

One accepts or encourages political, social and economic structures which urge conflict, ultimately armed conflict, and when the conflict breaks out one sees the guilt in the persons of the politicians or the military instead of in the pressure of the system from which these people, with the best will in the world, can scarcely extricate themselves. One allows oneself a spiritual attitude filled with anxiety and aggression and is shocked by the inevitable battles which a society of people with such attitudes produces. A will to peace, which does not see the social and spiritual causes of war, is not a real change of consciousness; it is as it were simply a symbol of longing for such change.[9]

The situation of mankind is now so complicated that the steps recommended by the peace researchers to change people's awareness cannot affect large sections of the population within a foreseeable period – quite apart from the fact that there is controversy even among the peace researchers and a general lack of authority to back up valuable new discoveries. So let us turn to the prophecies of the religions on their apocalyptic expectations and the appearance of the Prince of Peace. Here it must be stated quite clearly and unambiguously that *Apocalypse* does not mean the end of all time, the end of the world and of history, but the *end of an age*. According to the Bible it is not the *cosmos* that ends but the *aeon*, which translates as 'age'. A new *age* is beginning, which will be described as the age of *maturity* and of fulfilment.

Zarathustra proclaims the coming of Shah-Bahram. In his day the ultimate victory of good over evil will be won and his era will be an era of peace. In the Old Testament this key truth is transmitted in a number of metaphors: 'The sucking child shall play on the hole of the asp', 'the wolf also shall dwell with the lamb'. The promised Tenth Avatar of the Hindus and the expected Fifth Buddha are peace-bringers. According to Islamic tradition, the coming of the Mahdi or Qá'im will introduce a period in which justice will ultimately prevail on earth. In Christianity they speak of the establishment of the Kingdom of God on earth, of a new heaven and a new earth, of the City of God, of the new Jerusalem, of God coming down from heaven, of the meek inheriting the earth. Symbols, allegories and metaphors, all saying the same thing. It is a time characterised by the grace of a new beginning, a new day, introduced by a Prince of Peace – that day is the day of God. Whereas the dispensation of Jesus is identified with the dispensation of the Son, the dispensation of the Prince of Peace is equated with the dispensation of the Father. He is the Lord of the vineyard.

The idea of peace is so strongly identified with the coming of the Lord that the German Bishops stated in 1983, at the Bishops' Conference on Peace: 'Eucharist and Sunday make up a single unit. Sunday thus becomes a foreshadowing of the perfect peace which the Lord will bestow on the world when He returns.'[10]

Vatican II comes to the same view: 'Inasmuch as men

are sinners, the peril of war threatens them and will continue to threaten them until the Coming of Christ. But inasmuch as men unite in love and thus overcome sin, so also they overcome violence.'[11]

For Bahá'ís the cornerstone of peace is the certainty that Bahá'u'lláh is the promised Prince of Peace, the Shah-Bahram, the Fifth Buddha, the Tenth Avatar, the Mahdi and the Second Coming of Christ.

The result of this is a firmly anchored assurance of peace which cannot be disappointed by strife and war, or by the downfall of mankind in the melting pot of suffering as a necessary purification in the process of reaching maturity for peace. To commit themselves to this end is worth any sacrifice to Bahá'ís. Since, however, Bahá'ís live in an unqualified faith in peace, because for them the promised day has dawned, they are really the fortunate, the richly endowed ones, already breathing the pure air of this unity of mankind, because they have recognised the task and goal of their lives in realising it here and now.

In connection with all these promises, the time has come to affirm that we need a *new faith*, which theology can no longer bring us. More is *required* today. We must dare to make a *new beginning*. We must beware lest, in the name of Christ, in the name of the Son, we resist the Father.

In conclusion, let the promise be set against the claim: the promise originates with John of Patmos, from the Revelation that bears his name, and mentions the new name of Bahá'u'lláh. The claim is taken from the writings of Bahá'u'lláh known as the 'Tablet of Carmel':

And I saw a new heaven and a new earth; for the first heaven and the first earth were passed away; and there was no more sea. And I saw the Holy City, new Jerusalem, coming down from God out of heaven . . . And I heard a great voice from the throne, saying: Behold, the tabernacle of God is with men and He will dwell with them and they shall be His people, and God Himself shall be with them . . . And the city has no need of the sun, neither of the moon, to shine in it; for the Glory of God[12] doth lighten it and the Lamb is the light thereof. And the nations shall walk in the light of it; and the kings of the earth bring their glory into it. And the gates of it shall not be shut by day; for there shall be no night there.[13]

Bahá'u'lláh writes:

Call out to Zion, O Carmel, and announce the joyful tidings: He that was hidden from mortal eyes is come! His all-conquering sovereignty is manifest; His all-encompassing splendour is revealed. Beware lest thou hesitate or halt . . . Oh, how I long to announce unto every spot on the surface of the earth, and to carry to each one of its cities, the glad tidings of this Revelation – a Revelation to which the heart of Sinai hath been attracted and in whose name the Burning Bush is calling: 'Unto God, the Lord of Lords, belong the kingdoms of earth and heaven.' Verily this is the Day in which both land and sea rejoice at this announcement, the Day for which have been laid up those things which God, through a bounty beyond the ken of mortal mind or heart, hath destined for revelation. Ere long will God sail His Ark upon thee and will manifest the people of Bahá who have been mentioned in the Book of Names.

APPENDIX

They Were Moved

Edward G. Browne (1862–1926): The Encounter

One of the few Europeans who came into Bahá'u'lláh's presence was the English orientalist Edward G. Browne of Cambridge University. Of his impressions of a visit in 1890, two years before Bahá'u'lláh's passing, Browne writes:

My conductor paused for a moment while I removed my shoes. Then, with a quick movement of the hand, he withdrew, and, as I passed, replaced the curtain; and I found myself in a large apartment, along the upper end of which ran a low divan, while on the side opposite to the door were placed two or three chairs. Though I dimly suspected whither I was going and whom I was to behold (for no distinct intimation had been given to me), a second or two elapsed ere, with a throb of wonder and awe, I became definitely conscious that the room was not untenanted. In the corner where the divan met the wall sat a wondrous and venerable figure, crowned with a felt head-dress of the kind called *táj* by dervishes (but of unusual height and make), round the base of which was wound a small white turban. The face of him on whom I gazed I can never forget, though I cannot describe it. Those piercing

eyes seemed to read one's very soul; power and authority sat
on that ample brow; while the deep lines on the forehead and
face implied an age which the jet-black hair and beard flowing
down in indistinguishable luxuriance almost to the waist
seemed to belie. No need to ask in whose presence I stood, as I
bowed myself before one who is the object of a devotion and
love which kings might envy and emperors sigh for in vain!

A mild dignified voice bade me be seated, and then
continued:- 'Praise be to God that thou hast attained! . . .
Thou hast come to see a prisoner and an exile . . . We desire
but the good of the world and the happiness of the nations; yet
they deem us a stirrer up of strife and sedition worthy of
bondage and banishment . . . That all nations should become
one in faith and all men as brothers; that the bonds of affection
and unity between the sons of men should be strengthened;
that diversity of religion should cease, and differences of race
be annulled – what harm is there in this? . . . Yet so it shall be;
these fruitless strifes, these ruinous wars shall pass away, and
the 'Most Great Peace' shall come . . . Do not you in Europe
need this also? Is not this that which Christ foretold? . . . Yet
do we see your kings and rulers lavishing their treasures more
freely on means for the destruction of the human race than on
that which would conduce to the happiness of mankind . . .
These strifes and this bloodshed and discord must cease, and
all men be as one kindred and one family . . . Let not a man
glory in this, that he loves his country; let him rather glory in
this, that he loves his kind . . .'[1]

Leo Tolstoy (1828–1910)

In January 1904 a play by the Russian poet Isabella
Grinevskaya was performed in St. Petersburg (now
Leningrad). The subject of this successful drama, entitled
The Báb, was the personality, teaching and martyrdom
of the Herald of the Bahá'í Faith and became the talk of
the town in the literary, artistic and intellectual circles of

Russia and Western Europe. The play was frequently performed even after the Revolution.

After reading the play, Tolstoy wrote the author a letter of appreciation which also appeared in the Press. Here is a short extract:

. . . the Bábí teachings, insofar as they reject the old Muslim superstitions . . . and hold fast to their main and fundamental ideas of brotherhood, equality and love, are assured of a great future . . . I sympathise with all my heart with Bábism, insofar as it preaches brotherhood and equality between all men, and the sacrifice of material life in the service of God.[2]

Tolstoy would discuss the Bahá'í teachings (which he knew under the name 'Bábism') with correspondents and visitors, among them the German poet Rainer Maria Rilke who on his return from Moscow sent Tolstoy a pamphlet about the new faith.[3] Publicly, Tolstoy involved himself with the Bahá'í Faith when the Persian Ambassador in St. Petersburg, who had attended the World Peace Conference in The Hague in 1899, sent him a poem on peace. Tolstoy replied to the effect that it was not governments which would put an end to wars on earth, complaining at the same time that the Persian government was persecuting the Bahá'ís (Bábís) whom he regarded as the followers of the true religion.[4]

Over the years Tolstoy came to read more and more about the Bahá'í Faith. On the advice of 'Abdu'l-Bahá, then a prisoner in 'Akká, an Iranian Bahá'í visited him at his country estate where he was virtually under house arrest at the time. Tolstoy corresponded with several other Bahá'ís and from various sources we learn that he intended to write a book about the Bahá'í Faith. In a letter to a young student in Moscow Tolstoy wrote: 'Bábism, which has evolved into Bahá'ism (Bahá'u'lláh), and which has its roots in Islám, is one of the highest and purest of religious teachings.'[5]

'Very profound. I know of no other so profound,' was his comment on the Bahá'í teachings a few months before his death.[6]

'We spend our lives', Tolstoy is reported to have written elsewhere, 'attempting to unlock the secret of the universe. There was once a Turkish prisoner, who had the key.'[7]

Qurratu'l-'Ayn (Táhirih) (1817– 1852)[8]

The manner in which Táhirih accepted the Báb, the Herald of the Bahá'í Faith, recalls the story of the Three Kings who were led by the Star to Jesus's birthplace. She had the conviction that the time was fulfilled. Her guiding star was her sister's husband, who like herself belonged to the Shaykhí Movement.[9] She entrusted a letter to him, to be handed to the Awaited One as soon as he met Him and recognised Him. She believed in the new Divine Revealer without ever having met Him, without external proofs. Her poems demonstrate that she too had recognised the station of Bahá'u'lláh long before He proclaimed His mission. She was accepted by the Báb into the ranks of the first apostles, the only woman among eighteen.

Táhirih came from a respected family in Qazvin. Her father and uncle were the leading Islamic clergy of the town. Even in her early childhood Táhirih was remarkable for her intelligence, eloquence and thirst for knowledge. She is regarded as the most important woman poet Persia has ever produced and at the same time she made an important contribution to the emancipation of women. At a historic conference in Badasht, a north Persian village, in 1848, where 81 followers of the Báb discussed the future of the community, she appeared unveiled and gave a passionate speech on the meaning of the new Revelation. She made a dual impression: firstly, by throwing off the symbol of female inferiority she symbolised the new age of the equality of the sexes; secondly, she demonstrated impressively that in the new Dispensation the old laws of Islam had lost their validity and new ones had taken their place. The effect of her action was so shocking that some of the faithful abandoned the new faith for ever. The symbol of purity, the re-embodiment of the divine Fatima, had been dishonoured in their eyes. In this connection Bahá'u'lláh described her as Táhirih (Pure One), an honorific which confirms both her personal immaculacy and the rightness of her motivation and action.

During the Bábí persecutions of that time Táhirih was imprisoned in the house of the Mayor of Teheran. The Shah of the day offered to receive her at Court – she was an extremely beautiful woman – if she would abjure her faith. She replied in a poem, an outstanding example of Persian lyricism of that age, in which she informed the despot that she preferred a life of uncertainty and affliction to the proffered life of pomp and splendour. She even had a presentiment of her martyrdom. She took leave of the family of the Mayor, by whom she was by now greatly revered; and in expectation of her fate she donned her bridal robe and became absorbed in prayer and worship. At a late hour she was led to a garden oustide the town and throttled with her own scarf. A

Western eye-witness, later the Shah's personal physician, Dr Jakob E. Polak, wrote: 'I witnessed the execution of Qurratu'l-'Ayn, which was carried out by the War Minister and his adjutant; the beautiful woman endured her slow death with superhuman strength.'[10]

'The heroism of the lovely but ill-fated poetess of Qasvín, Zarrín-Táj (Crown of Gold) . . .' testifies Lord Curzon of Kedleston, 'is one of the most affecting episodes in modern history.' 'The appearance of such a woman as Qurratu'l-'Ayn', wrote the well-known British Orientalist, Prof. E. G. Browne, 'is, in any country and in any age, a rare phenomenon, but in such a country as Persia it is a prodigy – nay, almost a miracle . . . had the Bábí religion no other claim to greatness, this were sufficient . . . that it produced a heroine like Qurratu'l-'Ayn.'[11]

George Townshend (1876–1957)

'And I saw a new heaven and a new earth.' So runs the inscription on the gravestone of the former Anglican clergyman, Canon of St. Patrick's Cathedral, Dublin, and Archdeacon of Clonfert. George Townshend[12] first encountered the Bahá'í Faith in 1916 and became one of its foremost apologists. His books were written to help seeking Christians to come closer to the new faith from a Christian standpoint.[13] When he renounced his orders he said that he did so 'in order to be loyal to Christ as I know Him'. Soon afterwards he wrote a public letter to fellow Christians everywhere, urgently requesting them to take Bahá'u'lláh's claim seriously and make an impartial investigation of the Bahá'í Faith:

Having identified myself with the Faith of Bahá'u'lláh and

sacrificed my position as a canon and a dignitary of the Church of Ireland to do so, I now make this statement on the relation of this Faith to Christianity and to the Churches of Christ.

It is submitted to all Christian people in general but more especially to the bishops and clergy and members of my own communion, with the humble but earnest and urgent request that they will give it their attention as a matter of vital concern to the Church. Only through an impartial investigation of the Cause of Bahá'u'lláh will they find, I fully believe, a means of reviving the fortunes of the Church, of restoring the purity and the power of the Gospel and of helping to build a better and more truly Christian world.[14]

The response to his appeal was meagre. Insofar as any Prince of the Church reacted at all, or replied from sheer politeness, his answer was restricted to the statement that Bahá'u'lláh was not really saying anything new. Townshend was more pitied than taken seriously.

George Townshend came from a distinguished Irish family, but his profession of faith brought him isolation and poverty. To the end of his life he busied himself trying to make his conviction comprehensible to an indifferent world. In his last book, published shortly before his death, he once more appealed to his fellow Christians not to reject out of hand the message of Bahá'u'lláh:

The Bahá'í Faith today presents the Christian Churches with the most tremendous challenge ever offered them in their long history: a challenge, and an opportunity. It is the plain duty of every earnest Christian in this illumined Age to investigate for himself with an open and fearless mind the purpose and the teachings of this Faith and to determine whether the collective centre for all the constructive forces of this time be not the Messenger from God, Bahá'u'lláh, He and no other; and whether the way to a better, kinder, happier world will not lie open as soon as we accept the Announcement our rulers rejected.[15]

Queen Marie of Romania (1857–1938)

She was the eldest daughter of the Duke of Edinburgh, Queen Victoria's second son, and the granddaughter of Czar Alexander II. Both Queen Victoria and the Czar had received letters personally addressed to them by Bahá'u'lláh. By birth and marriage Queen Marie was related to the major ruling families of Europe. Born in the Anglican faith, she was intimately associated by marriage with the Greek Orthodox Church. She was a very gifted writer, of winning personality, well-known for her works of charity, her courage and energy. After learning of the Bahá'í Faith through Martha Root[16] and having appreciated the significance of Bahá'u'lláh's message through personal study, she did not hesitate to declare her faith in Bahá'u'lláh. In countless statements to her relations and the public as a whole she fearlessly testified to her new faith. She tried to make a pilgrimage to the holy places of the Bahá'í Faith in Haifa and 'Akká, but to her regret her plan was prevented by reasons of state. On 27 August 1926 Queen Marie wrote from Bran to the Guardian of the Bahá'í Faith, Shoghi Effendi:

Dear Sir,
   I was deeply moved on reception of your letter.
   Indeed a great light came to me with the message of Bahá'u'lláh and Abdu'l-Bahá. It came as all great messages come at an hour of dire grief and inner conflict and distress, so the seed sank deeply.

My youngest daughter finds also great strength and comfort in the teachings of the beloved masters.

We pass on the message from mouth to mouth and all those we give it to see a light suddenly lighting before them and much that was obscure and perplexing becomes simple, luminous and full of hope as never before.

That my open letter was balm to those suffering for the cause, is indeed a great happiness to me, and I take it as a sign that God accepted my humble tribute.

The occasion given me to be able to express myself publically, was also His Work, for indeed it was a chain of circumstances of which each link led me unwittingly one step further, till suddenly all was clear before my eyes and I understood why it had been.

Thus does He lead us finally to our ultimate destiny.

Some of those of my caste wonder at and disapprove my courage to step forward pronouncing words not habitual for Crowned Heads to pronounce, but I advance by an inner urge I cannot resist.

With bowed head I recognize that I too am but an instrument in greater Hands and rejoice in the knowledge.

Little by little the veil is lifting, grief tore it in two. And grief was also a step leading me ever nearer truth, therefore do I not cry out against grief!

May you and those beneath your guidance be blessed and upheld by the sacred strength of those gone before you.[17]

She repeatedly declared her support for the Bahá'í Faith to the public, for instance in the *Toronto Daily Star* of 4 May 1926:

If ever the name of Bahá'u'lláh or 'Abdu'l-Bahá comes to your attention, do not put their writings from you. Search out their Books, and let their glorious, peace-bringing, love-creating words and lessons sink into your hearts as they have into mine . . . Seek them, and be the happier.

August Forel (1848–1931)

His portrait adorns the 1,000-franc note of the Swiss National Bank. Forel, world-renowned psychiatrist, entomologist, anatomist and social reformer can be rightly regarded as one of Switzerland's most important sons. His work and writings, which went into large impressions and were translated into many languages, cover a very broad range of subjects.[18]

He was a pioneer of the temperance movement, of adult education and training, of women's rights, of penal reform; tireless in his efforts for peace. He was a monist when he encountered the new faith. Forel's humanist consciousness was so stirred by the doctrines of the Bahá'í Faith that he did not hesitate to adopt it, as he expressly stated and emphasised on various occasions.[19] Even then a wave of suppression was surging against the Bahá'í community in Iran. Forel intervened with the authorities to the best of his ability in order to ease the lot of his co-religionists.

One of 'Abdu'l-Bahá's weightiest letters was addressed to August Forel. In it he explores the conflict between those who believe in God, on the one hand, and the materialists and atheists, on the other, and sensitively presents proofs of the existence of intelligence and will beyond the universe of the senses.[20]

Forel asked that his last Will be read out beside the open grave. In it he writes:

At Karlsruhe, in 1920, I first came to know of the supraconfessional world religion of the Bahá'ís, founded in the East more than seventy-five years ago by the Persian Bahá'u'lláh. This is the true religion of the human social good, without dogma or priests, uniting all men on this small terrestrial globe of ours. I have become a Bahá'í. May this religion live and prosper for the good of mankind; this is my most ardent wish.[21]

Lidia Zamenhof (1904–1944)

Her father, the Polish oculist Ludwik Lazarus Zamenhof (1859–1917), was the inventor of Esperanto. Lidia was his youngest daughter.[22] At nine she learned Esperanto in six weeks, when it was thought that she might have to be left alone with relations in Warsaw during the Berne Esperanto Congress. In 1925 she successfully completed her law studies. Ludwik Zamenhof knew of the Bahá'í Faith and valued it highly. In 1911 he had already written to the Universal Race Congress in London on the necessity for a universal religion. Relations between Esperantists and Bahá'ís have always been cordial, with Bahá'ís speaking at many Esperanto Congresses, especially because the introduction of an auxiliary world language besides the mother tongue is one of Bahá'u'lláh's essential demands.

At the annual Esperanto Congresses Lidia Zamenhof learned the Bahá'í philosophy and through long personal acquaintance with the outstanding Bahá'í teacher Martha Root became a Bahá'í in 1928.

An imaginative and gifted writer and teacher, she became known for speaking out boldly for international co-operation and peace, for human unity and the equality of men and women. She devoted considerable time to the translation of important Bahá'í writings into Esperanto, including Esslemont's standard work *Bahá'u'lláh and the New Era*, but her intensive Bahá'í activities displeased relations and friends and in order to appease them she translated *Quo Vadis?* by Sienkiewicz and novellas by B. Prus into Esperanto, still without reducing her Bahá'í work. In 1937 she went to the USA where she performed great services to Bahá'í teaching and the dissemination of Esperanto. Only at the end of November 1938, when the political situation in Poland worsened, did Lidia return to her family. During the German occupation the members of the Jewish Zamenhof family were imprisoned one by one. Lidia, in the Warsaw ghetto, was cut off from the outside world. She died in the Treblinka gas chambers in 1944.

Mark Tobey (1890–1976)

Mark Tobey[23] occupies a special position in the history of art. Inspired in the most important period of his artistic creativity by the reviving impulses of religion, he was consequently also controversial, finding enthusiastic support on the one hand and total rejection on the other. In 1918 Mark Tobey became a Bahá'í, enriching his artistic range through acquaintance with Chinese painting and calligraphy. Trips to Paris, Spain, Greece and the Near East extended his artistic work. From 1930 onwards Tobey was for a time Artist-in-residence at Dartington Hall, a progressive school in Devonshire. Here he met leading intellectual figures such as Aldous Huxley, Rabindranath Tagore and Arthur Waley, while artists such as Bernard Leach the potter came to the Bahá'í Faith through him. Tobey also paid visits to China and Japan, where he spent some time in a Zen monastery in order to make an intensive study of philosophy and the technique of Far Eastern calligraphy. From 1939 on, important American galleries became interested in Tobey's works. In 1952 a film was made about him, in which the idea of unity in the Bahá'í sense occupies a central position. The film was shown at the Edinburgh and Venice Festivals.

In 1958 Mark Tobey was awarded the first prize at the Venice Biennale, a distinction only once given to an American in this century. His move to Basle was followed by many honours, including an exhibition of 300 works at the Louvre (such a distinction had never before been accorded to a non-French living artist). Mark Tobey received many international prizes, including the National Prize of the USA in 1956 and the Guggenheim International Award.

In 1958 he won the 'Art in America' first prize. In 1969 he was appointed to the American Academy of Arts and Sciences, but did not take up the appointment.

Mark Tobey was also a gifted musician and writer, some of whose articles were published in the Bahá'í magazine *World Order*. Besides his artistic activities he devoted his time to the Bahá'í cause, serving as a member of the National Spiritual Assembly in England and as Chairman of the local Spiritual Assembly in Basle for sixteen years.

In Mark Tobey, according to a consensus of his critics, some of the central ideas of the Bahá'í Faith took impressive shape as works of art.

Richard Edward St. Barbe Baker (1889–1982)

Even when he was still a child in Hampshire, St. Barbe Baker was interested in trees and everything connected with a healthy ecology. He studied forestry and theology and from 1921 onwards spent nine years in Africa, especially in Kenya and Nigeria, where he was concerned with the maintenance and nurture of the forests. He founded the society of the Men of the Trees in 1922 in Kenya, in 1924 in great Britain, in 1929 in Palestine and in 1932 as a worldwide society for the maintenance and nurture of trees. In 1956 St. Barbe Baker founded the Junior Men of the Trees for young people and in 1959 New Zealand became the home of the central office of the Men of the Trees in the Commonwealth and abroad.

He gave lectures and directed forest planning in the USA, Canada and South America. The Friends of the Sahara organisation owes its existence to him and it is thanks to him that the USA and Great Britain, together with 24 African countries, especially those bordering on the Sahara, became involved in a programme of reclamation and cultivation. Thousands of millions of trees have been planted all over the world on his initiative. He wrote thirty books on trees and the ecology, organised many exhibitions, and was the founder and publisher of the journal *Trees and Life*.

St. Barbe Baker heard about the Bahá'í Faith in 1924, studied the available books and became a Bahá'í. According to his own testimony, the Bahá'í Faith always remained the source of inspiration for his work. In his autobiography[24] he recounts how on his many journeys he always tried to make contact with the native Bahá'ís first, in order to pray with them before pursuing his projects.

In 1977 he was honoured by the Queen of England, and Prince Charles, the heir to the throne, became the Patron of the Men of the Trees. The University of Saskatchewan annually awards a Men of the Trees prize in the name of St. Barbe Baker to an individual who has rendered outstanding services to plants and the ecology.

In his work all over the world St. Barbe Baker always did

his best to make use of the tree-planting traditions of individual countries. For the Africans he introduced the 'Dance of Trees' and in Israel he adopted the tradition of Tubi'shvat, where the whole population participates in annual tree-planting. In his autobiography he describes how unconventionally he always approached his goal. In Jerusalem he invited the Mufti, the Latin and Greek Orthodox patriarchs, the Bishop of Jerusalem and the Rector of the Hebrew University to a discussion. None of those invited knew that the others were coming and it was the first time that the heads of the various religious communities had met. He told them that Palestine had once been covered with plants and it was now their common task to restore the conditions of the past. He won them all over to his project and all became members of Men of the Trees.

We can understand the life and work of St. Barbe Baker from his own words:

'I believe in the Oneness of Mankind and all living things and the interdependence of each and all.' 'I pray that I may be just to the Earth beneath my feet, to the neighbour by my side and to the light that comes from above and within, that this wonderful world of ours may be a little more beautiful and happy for my having lived in it.' 'I have a dream of the whole earth made green again, an earth healed and made whole through the efforts of children of all ages and all nations planting trees to express their special understanding of the earth as their home and of all children as their brothers and sisters'.

BIBLIOGRAPHY

'Abdu'l-Bahá. *Selections from the Writings of 'Abdu'l-Bahá*. Haifa: Bahá'í World Centre 1978.

—— *Some Answered Questions*. Wilmette, Illinois: Bahá'í Publishing Trust, rev. edn 1981.

Alt, Franz. *Frieden ist möglich*. Munich: Piper-Verlag 1983. *Peace is Possible: The Politics of the Sermon on the Mount*. Schocken 1985.

—— & Heiner Geissler. *Frieden und Freiheit sind möglich: Das Streitgespräch Franz Alt mit Heiner Geissler* (Peace and Freedom are Possible: The Confrontation between Franz Alt and Heiner Geissler). Munich: Olzog-Verlag 1983.

Anders, Guinther. *Hiroshima ist überall* (Hiroshima is Everywhere). Munich: C. H. Beck-Verlag 1982.

Bahá'u'lláh. *Gleanings from the Writings of Bahá'u'lláh*. London: Bahá'í Publishing Trust 1949. Wilmette, Illinois: Bahá'í Publishing Trust, rev. edn 1963.

—— *Tablets of Bahá'u'lláh revealed after the Kitáb-i-Aqdas*. Haifa: Bahá'í World Centre 1978.

Battke, Achim. *Atomrüstung — christlich zu verantworten?* (Nuclear Armaments – a Christian Justification?). Dusseldorf: Patmos-Verlag 1982.

Becker, Werner. *Der Streit um den Frieden* (The Conflict over Peace). Munich: Piper-Verlag 1984.

Borné, Gerhard. *Bergpredigt und Frieden* (The Sermon on the Mount and Peace). Olten: Walter-Verlag 1982.

Butterworth, John. *A Book of Beliefs, Cults and New Faiths*. Elgin, Illinois: David C. Cook 1981.

Chouleur, Jacques, 'La Foi Mondiale Baha'ie: Religion Planetiare de l'Avenir?' (The Bahá'í World Faith: Planetary Religion of the Future?). *Annales Universitaries*, Vol. 1, No. 2, Avignon 1975.

Consultation: A Compilation. Research Department of the Universal House of Justice. Wilmette, Illinois: Bahá'í Publishing Trust 1980. Published in the UK as *The Heaven of Divine Wisdom*. London: Bahá'í Publishing Trust 1980.

Danesh, Hossain B. *The Violence-Free Society: A Gift for Our Children*. Bahá'í Studies, Vol. 6. Ottawa: Canadian Association for Studies on the Bahá'í Faith 1979.

Dustar, Farzin. *Ausweg aus der Krise – das Modell des Friedens* (The Way Out of the Crisis – the Model for Peace). Luxembourg: Horizonte Verlag 1985.

Dustar, Farah. *Weltfriede durch Beteiligung der Frauen* (World Peace through Women's Participation). Luxembourg: Horizonte Verlag 1985.

Esslemont, J. E. *Bahá'u'lláh and the New Era*. London: Bahá'í Publishing Trust, 4th rev. edn 1974.

Gebser, Jean. *Abendländische Wandlung: Abriss der Ergebnisse moderner Forschung. Ihre Bedeutung für Gegenwart und Zukunft* (Western Transformation: Outline of the Results of Modern Research. Their Significance for Present and Future). Berlin: Ullsteinbook No. 107, 1965.

—— *Ein Mensch zu sein* (On Being a Man). Bern 1974.

—— *In der Bewährung* (On Probation). Bern 1969.

—— *Ursprung und Gegenwart* (Origin and Present). Munich 1973.

Gerechtigkeit schafft Frieden (Justice makes Peace). Secretariat of the German Bishop's Conference, Kaiserstrasse 163, 5300 Bonn 1, 18 April 1983.

Hättich, Manfred. *Weltfrieden durch Friedfertigkeit?* (World Peace through Readiness for Peace?). Munich: Olzog-Verlag 1983.

Hahn, Peter. *Pro & Contra*. Wiesbaden: Coprint-Verlag 1984.

Hakim, Christine. *Les Bahá'ís ou Victoire sur la Violence* (The Bahá'ís or Victory over Violence). Lausanne: Favre 1982.

Hatcher, W. S. & J. D. Martin. *The Bahá'í Faith: The Emerging*

Global Religion. New York: Harper & Row 1984

Heckeroth, Egon. *Auf den Spuren eines neuen Zeitalters* (On the Tracks of a New Age). Munich: Hugendubel-Verlag 1982.

Huddleston, John. *The Earth is but One Country*. London: Bahá'í Publishing Trust 1976.

Hutten, Kurt. *Seher, Grübler, Enthusiasten* (Seers, Ponderers, Enthusiasts). Stuttgart: Quell-Verlag 1966.

Jaspers, Karl. *Die Atombombe und die Zukunft des Menschen* (The Atom Bomb and the Future of Mankind). Munich: Piper-Verlag 1982.

Lapide, Pinchas. *Die Bergpredigt – Utopie oder Programm?* (The Sermon on the Mount – Utopia or Political Progamme?). Mainz: Matthias-Grunewald-Verlag 1982.

The Local Spiritual Assembly: An Institution of the Bahá'í Administrative Order. (comp.) Research Department of the Universal House of Justice. Wilmette, Illinois: Bahá'í Publishing Trust 1970. Published in the UK as *Local Spiritual Assemblies*. London: Bahá'í Publishing Trust 1970.

Mühlschlegel, Peter. 'Der Fetisch Souveränität' (The Fetish of Sovereignty). *Bahá'í-Briefe*, Vol. 47, p. 16. Hofheim-Langenhain: Bahá'í Verlag 1984.

Nabíl-i-A'zam. *The Dawn-Breakers: Nabíl's Narrative of the Early Days of the Bahá'í Revelation.* Translated and edited by Shoghi Effendi. Wilmette, Illinois: Bahá'í Publishing Trust 1932.

Panahi, Badi. *Vorurteile, Rassismus, Antisemitismus, Nationalismus . . . in der Bundesrepublik heute* (Prejudice, Racism, Antisemitism, Nationalism . . . in the Federal Republic Today). Frankfurt: S. Fischer-Verlag 1980.

Pfister, Hermann, & Rosemarie Wolf. *Friedenspädagogik heute* (Peace Education Today). Waldkirch: Waldkircher Verlagagesellschaft 1972.

Rabbaní, Rúḥíyyih. *The Priceless Pearl*. London: Bahá'í Publishing Trust 1969.

Rinsche, Franz-Josef. *Nur so ist Frieden möglich: Franz Alts Traume und die menschliche Realität* (Only Thus is Peace Possible: Franz Alt's Vision and Human Reality). Stuttgart: Seewald-Verlag 1984.

Sabet, Huschmand. *Einheit der Menschheit, Friede auf Erden, Frucht einer Universalreligion? Briefe zu einem umstrittenen Buch* (The Oneness of Mankind, Peace on Earth, the Fruit of a World Religion? Answers to a Controversial Book). Stuttgart: Verum–Verlag 1968.

—— *The Heavens Are Cleft Asunder*. Oxford: George Ronald 1975.

Schaefer, Udo. *The Imperishable Dominion*. Oxford: George Ronald 1983.

—— *Bahá'í – Religion nach Mass?* (Bahá'í – Religion Made to Measure?). Stuttgart: Verum–Verlag 1970.

—— *Sekte oder Offenbarungsreligion? Zur religionswissenschaftlichen Einordnung des Bahá'í-Glaubens* (Sect or Revealed Religion? Towards a Classification of the Bahá'í Faith according to Religious Science). Hofheim-Langenhain: Bahá'í Verlag 1982.

Schell, Jonathan. *The Abolition*. New York: Knopf 1984.

—— *The Fate of the Earth*. New York: Avon Books 1982.

Shoghi Effendi. *Bahá'í Administration*. Wilmette, Illinois: Bahá'í Publishing Trust 1953.

—— *God Passes By*. Wilmette, Illinois: Bahá'í Publishing Trust 1944.

—— *The Promised Day Is Come*. Wilmette, Illinois: Bahá'í Publishing Trust, rev. edn 1980.

—— *The World Order of Bahá'u'lláh*. Wilmette, Illinois: Bahá'í Publishing Trust, 2nd rev. edn 1974.

Spiegel, Peter. *Gedanken des Friedens – Die Reden und Schriften von 'Abdu'l-Bahá für eine neue Kultur des Friedens*. (Thoughts about Peace – Talks and Writings of 'Abdu'l-Bahá for a New Civilisation of Peace). Luxembourg: Horizonte Verlag 1985.

Star of the West. A Bahá'í Magazine, 1910–1933. RP Oxford: George Ronald 1978.

To the Peoples of the World. See The Universal House of Justice.

Tyson, J. *World Peace and World Government: From Vision to Reality*. Oxford: George Ronald 1985.

Universal House of Justice, The. *The Promise of World Peace*. Haifa: Bahá'í World Centre 1985. Annotated edition *To the*

Peoples of the World. Ottawa: Association for Bahá'í Studies 1986.

Vader, John Paul. *For the Good of Mankind: August Forel and the Bahá'í Faith.* Oxford: George Ronald 1984.

Weizsäcker, Carl-Friedrich von. *Wege in der Gefahr* (Paths through the Peril). Munich 1979.

World Order. A Bahá'í Magazine. Wilmette, Illinois: National Spiritual Assembly of the Bahá'ís of the United States 1966–

NOTES

PREFACE

1 Some of the following publications on the Bahá'í Faith would make a useful introduction: J. E. Esslemont, *Bahá'u'lláh and the New Era*, London: Bahá'í Publishing Trust, 4th rev. edn 1974; John Huddleston, *The Earth is but One Country*, London, Bahá'í Publishing Trust 1976; John Ferraby, *All Things Made New*, London: Bahá'í Publishing Trust, rev. edn 1985; William Hatcher and Douglas Martin, *The Bahá'í Faith: The Emerging Global Religion*, New York: Harper & Row 1984; Mary Perkins and Philip Hainsworth, *The Bahá'í Faith*, London: Ward Lock Educational 1982; Huschmand Sabet, *The Heavens Are Cleft Asunder*, Oxford: George Ronald 1976; *Encyclopaedia Britannica*, 15th edn, Chicago 1974.

I. THE NEW ARK OF GOD

1 Bahá'u'lláh, *Gleanings*, 43:6. References to *Gleanings* in this book are given by section and paragraph.
2 John 16:13.
3 Schaefer, *Imperishable Dominion*, p.228.
4 *Star of the West*, Vol. IV, No. 11, p.191.
5 Isaiah 32: 17.
6 See Rev. 2: 17.
7 John 16: 12–13.
8 *Famiglia Christiana*, Rome, 8 January 1986.
9 In Germany many of these are responses to *Frieden ist möglich* (Peace is Possible) by Franz Alt; *Manfred Hättich, Weltfrieden durch Friedfertigkeit?*; Alt, *Frieden und Freiheit sind möglich; Das Streitgespräch Franz Alt mit Heiner Geissler*; Peter Hahn, *Pro & Contra*; Franz-Josef Rinsche, *Nur so ist Frieden möglich: Franz Alts Träume und die menschliche Realität*; Werner Becker, *Der Streit um den Frieden*. See also: Achim Battke, *Atomrüstung –*

christlich zu verantworten?; Hossain Danesh, in: Farzin Dustdar, *Ausweg aus der Krise – das Modell des Friedens*; Farah Dustdar, *Weltfriede durch Beteiligung der Frauen*; Pinchas Lapide, *Die Bergpredigt – Utopie oder Programm?*; Peter Spiegel, *Gedanken des Friedens – Die Reden und Schriften von 'Abdu'l-Bahá für eine neue Kultur des Friedens*; Carl-Friedrich von Weizsäcker, *Wege in der Gefahr*.

10 Bahá'u'lláh, *Tablets*, p. 171.
11 Shoghi Effendi, *Promised Day*, pp. 117–18.

2. WHY NOT CHRISTIANITY?

1 'He knows the world', comments Peter Levi, Oxford University's Professor of Poetry.
2 Quoted from Pfister & Wolf, *Friedenspädagogik heute*, p. 50.
3 Ibid. p. 9.
4 Quoted by Shoghi Effendi, *Promised Day*, p. 120. Bahá'u'lláh is quoting Matt. 4: 18–19.
5 *Die Atombombe und die Zukunft des Menschen*, pp. 485f.
6 Becker, *Der Streit um den Frieden*, p. 38.
7 Schell *Abolition*, pp. 157–8. cf. also pp. 89, 110, 129f.
8 Ibid. p. 71.
9 More details of this on pp. 91ff.
10 See on this topic Danesh, *Violence-Free Society*; Schaefer, *Imperishable Dominion*, ch. 12, 'The New Man'.
11 *Frieden ist möglich*, p. 82.
12 Isaiah 9 : 5.
13 'Abdu'l-Bahá, *Some Answered Questions*, ch. 29.
14 Ibid. This and the preceding quotation are in explanation of I Cor. 15: 22.
15 See my discussion of this in *The Heavens are Cleft Asunder*, pp. 110–18.
16 Hättich, *Weltfrieden durch Friedfertigkeit?*, p. 26.
17 Matt. 5: 48.
18 Further details on this topic in Schaefer, *Bahá'í – Religion nach Mass?*; Sabet, *Einheit der Menschheit*.
19 Rinsche, *Nur so ist Frieden möglich*, p. 110.
20 In Islam the world is divided into the Land of Islam (*dàr al-Islàm*) and the Land of War (*dàr al-harb*). This starting point makes it clear that a world that falls into two parts can never be one world. Holy War is the consequence of this division.
21 Borné, *Bergpredigt und Frieden*, p. 20.
22 The German Bishops, *Gerechtigkeit schafft Frieden*, pp. 30f, 38, 40, 41.
23 Hutten, *Seher, Grübler, Enthusiasten*, p. 316.

24 Ibid. p.317
25 Butterworth, *Beliefs, Cults and New Faiths*, p.47.
26 Hättich, *Weltfrieden durch Friedfertigkeit?*, p.18.
27 Ibid. pp.18f.
28 Ibid. pp.78f.
29 Ibid. p.84.
30 In most Bahá'í prayer books.
31 See Isaiah 32: 17.
32 Matson, *The Idea of Man*, p.11., cited in Danesh, *Violence-Free Society*, p.3.
33 Bahá'u'lláh, *Gleanings*, 147:2.
34 *World Order*, Autumn 1976.
35 'Abdu'l-Bahá quoted by J. E. Esslemont, *Bahá'u'lláh and the New Era*, p.180.
36 I. Cor. 4: 5.
37 I. Cor. 2: 7–11.
38 Bahá'u'lláh, *Gleanings*, 31.

3. WE ARE ALL IN THE SAME BOAT

1 Quoted in Alt, *Frieden ist möglich*, p.12.
2 Cf. Jean Gebser in the Bibliography. In *Auf den Spuren eines neuen Zeitalters* Egon Heckeroth gives a very useful description of the connections between the development of world consciousness and the emergence of the Bahá'í Faith.
3 Bahá'u'lláh, *Gleanings*, 112.
4 Ibid. 122.
5 Ibid. 112.
6 Alt, *Frieden ist möglich*, p.115.
7 See also the statements on pages 89–92.
8 Schell, *The Fate of the Earth*, p.161.

4. WORLD ORDER, A NECESSITY

1 Bahá'u'lláh, *Gleanings*, 99.
2 'Wer erdachte das Undenkbare?' (Who thought the Unthinkable?), *Die Zeit*, 15 October 1982.
3 Bahá'u'lláh, *Tablets*, p. 69.
4 Bahá'u'lláh, *Gleanings*, 163 : 2.
5 Ibid. 118: 2, 3, 6.
6 Becker, *Der Streit um den Frieden*, p.75.
7 Bahá'u'lláh, *Gleanings*, 61.

8 Ibid. 143: 3.

9 'Der Fetisch Souveränität'.

10 Tyson, *World Peace and World Government*, pp. 14, 98.

11 Schell, *The Fate of the Earth*, p.177.

12 As a non-governmental organisation with consultative status (1970) on the United Nations Economic and Social Council as well as with UNICEF, the Bahá'í International Community has taken a stand from the Bahá'í point of view on the various problems of mankind, in 43 documents covering the topics: human rights, education, disarmament, racial discrimination, equal rights for men and women, protection of the environment, drugs, world food, etc.

5. GRAPPLING WITH A DIFFICULT HERITAGE

1 Bahá'u'lláh, *Gleanings*, 117.

2 Foreword to *To the Peoples of the World*, p. xiii.

3 *The Promise of World Peace*, pp.17,1.

4 ibid. pp.12–13.

5 Foreword to *To the Peoples of the World*, p. xiii.

6 *The Promise of World Peace*, pp.13–14.

7 Ibid. p.13.

8 Panahi, *Rassismus*, p.13.

9 Ibid. p.23.

10 *The Promise of World Peace*, pp. 4–5.

11 Heckeroth, *Auf dem Spuren eines neuen Zeitalters*, p.335.

12 *The Promise of World Peace*, p.6.

13 Rom. 12:21.

14 'Abdu'l-Bahá, *Some Answered Questions*, p.159; 'Tablet to August Forel' in Vader, *For the Good of Mankind*, p.77; *Selections*, p.27.

15 *The Promise of World Peace*, pp.11–12.

16 Ibid. p.12.

17 Ibid. p.7.

18 Ibid. pp.19–20.

6. THY KINGDOM COME

1 *The Promise of World Peace*, p.20.

2 See *Persecution of the Bahá'ís in Iran: A 6-Year Campaign to Eliminate a Religious Minority*, New York: Bahá'í International Community 1985; Douglas Martin, *The Persecution of the Bahá'ís in Iran 1844–1944*, Bahá'í Studies Vol. 12/13, Ottawa: Association for Bahá'í Studies 1984.

3 The system and methods of the Spiritual Assemblies can be gathered from *The Local Spiritual Assembly: An Institution of the Bahá'í Administrative Order*, compiled by the Universal House of Justice, from the writings of Bahá'u'lláh, 'Abdu'l-Bahá and Shoghi Effendi, 1970.

4 The Bahá'ís are fully aware that they are still at the beginning of this development. These institutions of the Spiritual Assemblies will unfold in the course of time and take the name 'Houses of Justice' assigned to them by Bahá'u'lláh. See *Consultation: A Compilation*.

5 Shoghi Effendi, *Bahá'í Administration*, p.141.

6 Houses of Worship exist today in Australia, Germany, India, Panama, Samoa, Uganda and the United States.

7 An exception is made for donations for charitable purposes; contributions towards these are accepted from Bahá'ís and non-Bahá'ís alike.

8 See on this topic Hatcher and Martin, *The Bahá'í Faith: The Emerging Global Religion*; Becker, *Der Streit um den Frieden*, p.95.

9 Further details in Schaefer, *Sekte oder Offenbarungsreligion?*

10 See for example Chouleur, *'La Foi Mondiale Baha'ie: Religion Planetaire de L'Avenir?'*

11 Rev. 21: 5.

7. THY WILL BE DONE ON EARTH

1 Bahá'u'lláh, *Gleanings*, 156.

2 See Shoghi Effendi, *The World Order of Bahá'u'lláh*, p.39. Shoghi Effendi comments elsewhere: 'The seven rays of unity need not necessarily appear in this order. One fruit of the second may well be a world civilisation.' (*Directives from the Guardian*, New Delhi: Bahá'í Publishing Trust 1973, p.67.)

3 Hakim, *Les Bahá'íes ou Victoire sur la Violence*, pp.174–5.

4 John 14:6.

5 In my book *The Heavens Are Cleft Asunder* I cite examples on pp.112f. and explore the subject more deeply.

6 Küng, 'Dialog mit den Muslimen', *Die Zeit*, 29 March 1985.

7 Bahá'u'lláh, *Gleanings*, 24.

8 See Nabíl-i-A'zam, *The Dawn-Breakers*; Shoghi Effendi, *God Passes By*.

9 Von Weizsäcker, *Wege in der Gefahr*, p.111.

10 *Gerechtigkeit schafft Frieden*, p.61.

11 The 'ten commandments of peace', taken from the Letter to Soldiers 55, published by Katholisches Militärbischofsamt Bonn (78:6), quoted in Pfister and Wolf, *Friedenspädagogik heute*, p.75.

12 Bahá'u'lláh in Arabic.

13 Rev.21: 1–3, 23–5.
14 Bahá'u'lláh, *Gleanings*, 11: 4.

APPENDIX: THEY WERE MOVED

1 E. G. Browne, Introduction to *A Traveller's Narrative*, 1891, RP Wilmette: Bahá'í Publishing Trust 1975.
2 Leo Tolstoy, letter to Mme. Isabella Grinevskaya, quoted in Luigi Stendardo, *Leo Tolstoy and the Bahá'í Faith*, Oxford: George Ronald 1985, p.33.
3 Ibid. pp.18–19.
4 Ibid. pp.19–21.
5 Ibid. pp.26–31, 50, 51–2, 54.
6 Ibid. p.56.
7 See Martha L. Root, 'Count Leo Tolstoy and the Bahá'í Movement', in *The Bahá'í World*, Vol V, New York: Bahá'í Publishing Committee 1936.
8 Her life seized the imagination of nineteenth-century Europeans. She was described as 'The Persian Joan of Arc'; the actress Sarah Bernhardt wanted a play written about her; as early as 1874 Marie von Najmájer published a detailed although not entirely accurate assessment under the title *Gurret-ul-Ayn: Ein Bild aus Persiens Neuzeit*, Vienna: Verlag L. Rosner 1874, RP National Spiritual Assembly of the Bahá'ís of Austria 1981. For a life see Martha Root, *Ṭáhirih the Pure*, Karachi 1938, RP Los Angeles: Kalimát Press 1981.
9 An Islamic Adventist movement which expected the coming of the Promised One in 1844/AH 1260(Islamic Calendar), 1000 lunar years after the occultation of the twelfth Imam.
10 Jakob E. Polak, *Persien: Das Land und seine Bewohner,* Leipzig 1865, p.353.
11 Quoted from Shoghi Effendi, *God Passes By*, p.76.
12 For a life see David Hofman, *George Townshend*, Oxford: George Ronald 1983.
13 *The Heart of the Gospel*, Oxford: George Ronald 1972; *The Promise of All Ages*, Oxford: George Ronald 1972; *The Covenant, An Analysis*, Manchester: Bahá'í Publishing Trust 1950; *The Old Churches and the New World Faith*, 1947; *The Glad Tidings of Bahá'u'lláh*, Oxford: George Ronald 1975; *The Mission of Bahá'u'lláh and Other Literary Pieces*, Oxford, George Ronald 1976; *Christ and Bahá'u'lláh*, Oxford: George Ronald 1970.
14 *The Old Churches and the New World Faith*, quoted in Hofman, *George Townshend*, App.3.

15 Townshend, *Christ and Bahá'u'lláh*, p.116.

16 For further details see M. R. Garis, *Martha Root*, Wilmette: Bahá'í Publishing Trust 1983.

17 Quoted in Rúḥiyyih Rabbani, *The Priceless Pearl*, p.108.

18 'He published over 1,200 books, scientific publications and newspaper articles on almost every imaginable subject.' (Vader, *For the Good of Mankind*, p.2.) In addition to specialist contributions to psychiatry, Forel's works include: *Jugend, Evolution, Kultur und Narkose*, Munich 1908; *Die Rolle der Heuchelei, der Beschränktheit und der Unwissenheit in der landläufigen Moral*, Munich 1908; *Malthusianismus oder Eugenik*, Munich 1908; *Die Vereinigten Staaten der Erde: Ein Kulturprogramm*, Munich 1914; *Genug zerstört, wieder aufbauen*, Zurich 1916; *Der supranationale Friede*, 1916; *Die Zukunft des Strafrechts. Ethik der Zukunft*, 1921; *Der Weg zur Kultur*, Vienna 1924; *Der wahre Sozialismus der Zukunft*, Berlin 1926.

19 See Vader, *For the Good of Mankind*.

20 'Tablet to Forel', ibid. App. 1.

21 Ibid. p. 67.

22 For a life see Wendy Heller, *Lidia: The Life of Lidia Zamenhof, Daughter of Esperanto*, Oxford: George Ronald 1985.

23 *Mark Tobey: Art and Belief*, Oxford: George Ronald 1984.

24 Richard St. Barbe Baker, *My Life, My Trees*, London: Lutterworth Press 1970.

25 *Saskatoon Star Phoenix*, 18 June 1982.